The French
and Indian War

Recent Titles in
Greenwood Guides to Historic Events, 1500–1900

The Dreyfus Affair
Leslie Derfler

The War of 1812
David S. Heidler and Jeanne T. Heidler

The Atlantic Slave Trade
Johannes Postma

Manifest Destiny
David S. Heidler and Jeanne T. Heidler

American Railroads in the Nineteenth Century
Augustus J. Veenendaal

Reconstruction
Claudine L. Ferrell

The Spanish-American War
Kenneth E. Hendrickson, Jr.

The American Revolution
Joseph C. Morton

The French Revolution
Linda S. Frey and Marsha L. Frey

The French and Indian War

ALFRED A. CAVE

Greenwood Guides to Historic Events, 1500–1900
Linda S. Frey and Marsha L. Frey, Series Editors

GREENWOOD PRESS
Westport, Connecticut • London

Library of Congress Cataloging-in-Publication Data

Cave, Alfred A.
   The French and Indian war / Alfred A. Cave.
      p. cm.—(Greenwood guides to historic events, 1500–1900, ISSN 1538–442X)
   Includes bibliographical references and index.
   ISBN 0–313–32168–X (alk. paper)
      1. United States—History—French and Indian War, 1755–1763.   I. Title.
   II. Series.
E199.C38   2004
973.2′6—dc22   2003060416

British Library Cataloguing in Publication Data is available.

Library of Congress Catalog Card Number: 2003060416
ISBN: 0–313–32168–X
ISSN: 1538–442X

First published in 2004

Greenwood Press, 88 Post Road West, Westport, CT 06881
An imprint of Greenwood Publishing Group, Inc.
www.greenwood.com

Printed in the United States of America

The paper used in this book complies with the
Permanent Paper Standard issued by the National
Information Standards Organization (Z39.48–1984).

10 9 8 7 6 5 4 3 2 1

CONTENTS

Photo essay follows page 70.

SERIES FOREWORD

American statesman Adlai Stevenson stated that "We can chart our future clearly and wisely only when we know the path which has led to the present." This series, Greenwood Guides to Historic Events, 1500–1900, is designed to illuminate that path by focusing on events from 1500 to 1900 that have shaped the world. The years 1500 to 1900 include what historians call the Early Modern Period (1500 to 1789, the onset of the French Revolution) and part of the Modern Period (1789 to 1900).

In 1500, an acceleration of key trends marked the beginnings of an interdependent world and the posing of seminal questions that changed the nature and terms of intellectual debate. The series closes with 1900, the inauguration of the twentieth century. This period witnessed profound economic, social, political, cultural, religious, and military changes. An industrial and technological revolution transformed the modes of production, marked the transition from a rural to an urban economy, and ultimately raised the standard of living. Social classes and distinctions shifted. The emergence of the territorial and later the national state altered man's relations with and view of political authority. The shattering of the religious unity of the Roman Catholic world in Europe marked the rise of a new pluralism. Military revolutions changed the nature of warfare. The books in this series emphasize the complexity and diversity of the human tapestry and include political, economic, social, intellectual, military, and cultural topics. Some of the authors focus on events in U.S. history such as the Salem Witchcraft Trials, the American Revolution, the abolitionist movement, and the Civil War. Others analyze European topics, such as the Reformation and Counter Reformation and the French Revolution. Still others bridge cultures and continents by examining the voyages of discovery, the Atlantic slave trade, and the Age of Imperialism. Some focus on intellectual questions that have shaped the modern world, such as Darwin's *Origin of Species,* or on turning points, such as the Age of Romanticism. Others examine defining economic, religious, or legal events or issues such as the building of the railroads, the Second Great Awakening, and abolitionism. Heroes (e.g., Lewis and Clark), scientists (e.g., Darwin), military leaders (e.g., Napoleon), poets (e.g., Byron), stride across its pages. Many of these events were seminal in that they marked profound changes or turning points. The Scientific Revolution, for example, changed the way individuals viewed themselves and their world.

The authors, acknowledged experts in their fields, synthesize key events, set developments within the larger historical context, and, most important, present a well-balanced, well-written account that integrates the most recent scholarship in the field.

The topics were chosen by an advisory board composed of historians, high school history teachers, and school librarians to support the curriculum and meet student research needs. The volumes are designed to serve as resources for student research and to provide clearly written interpretations of topics central to the secondary school and lower-level undergraduate history curriculum. Each author outlines a basic chronology to guide the reader through often confusing events and a historical overview to set those events within a narrative framework. Three to five topical chapters underscore critical aspects of the event. In the final chapter the author examines the impact and consequences of the event. Biographical sketches furnish background on the lives and contributions of the players who strut across this stage. Ten to fifteen primary documents ranging from letters to diary entries, song lyrics, proclamations, and posters cast light on the event, provide material for student essays, and stimulate a critical engagement with the sources. Introductions identify the authors of the documents and the main issues. In some cases a glossary of selected terms is provided as a guide to the reader. Each work contains an annotated bibliography of recommended books, articles, CD-ROMs, Internet sites, videos, and films that set the materials within the historical debate.

These works will lead to a more sophisticated understanding of the events and debates that have shaped the modern world and will stimulate a more active engagement with the issues that still affect us. It has been a particularly enriching experience to work closely with such dedicated professionals. We have come to know and value even more highly the authors in this series and our editors at Greenwood, particularly Kevin Ohe. In many cases they have become more than colleagues; they have become friends. To them and to future historians we dedicate this series.

Linda S. Frey
University of Montana

Marsha L. Frey
Kansas State University

PREFACE

In *Montcalm and Wolfe,* Francis Parkman's great romantic history of the French and Indian War first published in 1884, we read these words from the journal of a French colonel, Louis Antoine de Bougainville: "It is an abominable kind of war. The very air we breathe is contagious of insensibility and hardness." While Parkman was well aware of this war's sickening brutality, he nonetheless, as a staunch Protestant son of New England, sought to endow it with moral purpose. He declared that the war represented the "strife of the past against the future; of the old against the new; of moral and intellectual torpor against moral and intellectual life; of barren absolutism against a liberty crude, incoherent, and chaotic, yet full of a prolific vitality." Parkman not only portrayed the French as reactionaries; he demonized France's Native American allies, declaring in one passage, "The glitter of their vicious eyes told of the devil within." The French and Indian War, in his view, was a struggle between authoritarianism and barbarism, represented by Catholic France and her savage Indian allies, and liberty and enlightenment, championed by Protestant Britain and her fractious American colonies. The British victory was thus a milestone in the steady upward progress of humanity. A French victory, by contrast, would have meant a step backward for all mankind.[1]

Parkman was an exceptionally gifted writer. The color and the narrative power of his work remain unmatched. But he was also both a chauvinist and a racist. Modern readers generally find neither his heroes nor his villains quite believable. Bougainville's stark vision of horror now seems far closer to the war's reality.

The French and Indian War is misnamed. Not all Native Americans were supporters of the French. Both the French and the British sought Indian allies. Both were often frustrated in dealing with Indian leaders who clearly understood the risks of involvement, and sought to balance their own need for access to European goods against those risks. The Indians were not mindless savages. They were proud and independent peoples caught in a cruel dilemma. As to the matter of savagery, we now understand that in the course of this war, Englishmen and Frenchmen as well as Indians committed the "unspeakable" atrocities Parkman attributed mostly to Indians.

This war was not a moral crusade. It was a struggle for power, part of a worldwide war waged between two eighteenth-century superpowers. Its outcome in North America had an enormous impact on the future of both the winners and the losers. For Native American peoples, the elimination of France as a power in North America removed a vital counterweight against British expansionism and opened the way to their dispossession. For Great Britain, the war exposed crucial weaknesses in the structure of the empire. Efforts to repair those weaknesses led to a chain of blunders, misunderstandings, and confrontations that would culminate in the American Revolution. For France, the financial burdens and the military defeats incurred in waging the Seven Years' War (the name for the larger conflict of which the so-called French and Indian War was a part) contributed to the weakening of the Old Regime and to the coming of the French Revolution. The effects of the French and Indian War are thus with us even today. Comprehension of the nature of this great conflict is essential to the understanding of the history of the modern world.

This book offers an introduction to the study of the French and Indian War. At the beginning, a chronology traces the major events. The first chapter provides a narrative overview of the action, followed by four interpretive essays which analyze the interactions of Native Americans, French settlers, British colonials, and imperial officials. A concluding essay explores the long-term consequences of the war. A chapter of biographical sketches introduces the reader to some of the major players. A collection of excerpts from primary source documents affords the reader eyewitness testimony from French, British, and Indian perspectives. The annotated bibliography surveys the scholarly literature, offering many suggestions for further reading.

Note

1. Francis Parkman, *Montcalm and Wolfe* (New York: Da Capo Press, 1995), 20, 244, 251.

CHRONOLOGY OF EVENTS

1689–97 King William's War (The Nine Years' War)

1702–13 Queen Anne's War (War of the Spanish Succession)

1744–48 King George's War (War of the Austrian Succession)

1749 Captain Pierre-Joseph Céleron de Blainville's tour of the Ohio country

1753 The French begin to construct forts in contested western territories

1754, May 28 Virginia militia commanded by George Washington attack a French army detachment in western Pennsylvania

1754, June 14–July 11 The Albany Congress tries to renew the British alliance with the Iroquois and discusses Benjamin Franklin's Plan of Union

1754, July 4 Washington surrenders to the French at Fort Necessity

1755, February 23 General Edward Braddock arrives in Virginia to take command of the campaign against the French

1755, June 16–17 New England militia troops in Nova Scotia capture forts Beausejour and Gaspereau on the contested border with New France

1755, July 9 Braddock's defeat and subsequent death in western Pennsylvania

1755, September 8 William Johnson's forces turn back a French attack near Crown Point, New York, capturing the French commander, Baron Ludwig Dieskau

1755, October 13 The British deport over 10,000 Acadians (French residents of Nova Scotia)

1756, March In response to the French invasion of Minorca in the Mediterranean, Great Britain declares war on France

1756, July 22 John Campbell, Lord Loudoun, arrives in New York City and takes command of British and colonial forces

1756, August Delaware Indian raiders destroy Fort Granville, Pennsylvania

1756, August 14 The French capture Fort Oswego

1757, August 9 Fort William Henry surrenders to General Louis Montcalm. A number of British and colonial prisoners are subsequently massacred by Indians allied with the French

1757, December William Pitt recalls Lord Loudoun; General James Abercromby is appointed supreme commander

1758, July 8 Abercromby's attack on Fort Carillon (Ticonderoga) repulsed by Montcalm

1758, July 26 Louisbourg captured by General Jeffrey Amherst

1758, August 24 Fort Frontenac surrenders to John Bradstreet

1758, November 24 The French abandon Fort Duquesne; General John Forbes occupies the forks of the Ohio

1758, Fall The Indians of the Ohio valley make peace with the British

1759 The League of the Iroquois agrees to support the British war effort

1759, July 9 The French surrender Fort Niagara and lose all water access to the west

1759, July 27 Pressed by Amherst's forces, the French blow up Fort Carillon and evacuate their outposts on Lake Champlain

1759, September 13 General James Wolfe and Montcalm are fatally wounded in the battle for Quebec

1759, September 18 Quebec surrenders

1759, November 22 The French navy suffers a disastrous defeat in the battle of Quiberon Bay, in France

1759–1760 The Anglo-Cherokee War

1760, May French General Francois de Levis's efforts to recapture Quebec fail

1760, September 8 Montreal falls; Governor Pierre Vaudreuil surrenders all of New France

1763 The Peace of Paris ends the Seven Years' War in Europe and confirms France's loss of Canada

1763–1765 Pontiac's War

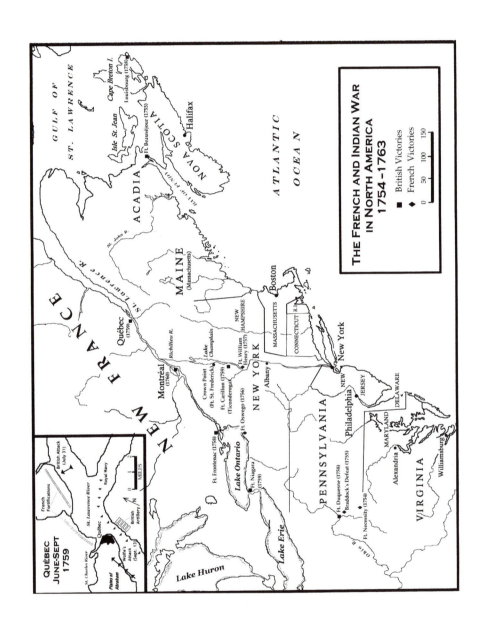

THE FRENCH AND INDIAN WAR
IN NORTH AMERICA
1754-1763

■ British Victories
◆ French Victories

0 50 100 150

OJIBWAYS

Lake Superior

Québec

Port Royal

Ottawa River Montréal

ABNAKIS

Lake Huron

St. Lawrence River

OTTAWAS

Lake Michigan

MOHAWKS

ONEIDAS

Lake Ontario **TUSCARORAS**

ONANDAGAS

Connecticut River

Boston

WYANDOTS

CAYUGAS

WINNEBAGOS

Lake Erie

SENECAS

KICKAPOOS

MINGOS

WESTERN DELAWARES

EASTERN DELAWARES

Hudson River

New York

Philadelphia

MIAMIS

SHAWNEES

Ohio River

Monongahela River

Potomac River

ATLANTIC

OCEAN

Mississippi River

Tennessee River

New Bern

CHEROKEES

Savannah River

Charleston

UPPER CREEKS

LOWER CREEKS

Savannah

St. Augustine

New Orleans

GULF OF MEXICO

**INDIANS OF EASTERN
NORTH AMERICA
DURING THE
FRENCH AND INDIAN WAR**

0   150   300

Miles

CHAPTER 1

Overview of the French and Indian War

On a backwoods trail in western Pennsylvania in the summer of 1758, a Delaware Indian the colonists called Daniel cursed both England and France. "Damn you!" he exclaimed to a British emissary, "why do not you and the French fight on the sea? You come here only to cheat the Indians and take their land from them."[1] As a survivor of a people driven from the eastern seaboard by land-hungry whites and forced to resettle in western villages hundreds of miles from their homeland, Daniel's distrust and his anger are understandable. His fear that the war would lead to further loss of Indian land proved to be all too well founded. But Daniel did not comprehend the scope of the conflict Americans would later name the French and Indian War. Known in European history as the Seven Years' War, it was fought not only on land but also on the high seas, and not only in North America, but in the Caribbean, Europe, Africa, and Asia as well. It was one of a long series of Anglo-French wars beginning in 1689 and not ending until 1815, wars fought not only for dominance in Europe but also for control of vast, intercontinental empires.

King William's War 1689–97

The first of those conflicts, the Nine Years' War (1688–97), was known in America as King William's War. In 1688, a number of European powers, including Austria, Spain, the United Provinces (Holland), Savoy, and several German states, alarmed by the expansionist ambitions of Louis XIV, had gone to war against France. England joined this anti-French alliance a year later. Although military action on this side of the Atlantic was limited to the frontier between French Canada and the English colonies, this war in its brutality foreshadowed the greater conflicts to come. Atrocities were committed by both sides, as English and French colonial raiding parties supported by Indian warriors burned farms and villages and murdered noncombatants on both sides of the border. New England's noted Indian fighter, Benjamin Church, called out of retirement to terrorize the Canadian frontier towns, related in his memoirs how in a raid on an Indian fort in New Brunswick, mounted while its warriors were away, he and his men had systematically clubbed to death their women and children.[2] The French and their Indian allies were no less ruthless, putting to the torch Schenectady, New York, Salmon Falls, and Falmouth, and killing scores of townspeople.

King William's War anticipated later North American wilderness wars in another respect. The English colonies under attack received little aid from one another, or from their more fortunate southern neighbors, as colonial assemblies ignored requests from the commander in chief sent by London to coordinate the war effort. An English official complained that despite their substantial numerical advantage over the French in Canada, the colonists "are so disunited in their interests that [they] have hitherto afforded but little assistance to each other."[3] On the French side, Louis XIV did not care to invest much in America, and ignored the pleas from his aggressive governor of New France, Count Louis Frontenac, that the attacks on British frontier settlements be supported by a naval assault on New York City. Had the king listened, one historian conjectures, "the story of Canada and the United States might have been very different."[4] As it was, the high point of King William's War in North America was the seizure in 1690 of the French stronghold of Port Royal in Acadia (Nova Scotia) by Massachusetts Governor Sir William Phips and his militia. The larger war ended in a stalemate. The Treaty of Ryswick returned Port Royal to France.

Queen Anne's War 1702–13

The War of the Spanish Succession (1702–13), known to the colonists as Queen Anne's War, originated in a dynastic controversy between the French ruling house, the Bourbons, and the Austrian Habsburgs. In 1700, Charles II, Habsburg king of Spain, died without an heir. He left his kingdom to Philip, duke of Anjou, youngest grandson of his enemy, King Louis XIV of France. Charles hoped that, through Bourbon assistance, the partition of Spanish Habsburg lands among various claimants could be averted. He added a provision that granted his realm to the Habsburg archduke Charles, son of Leopold I of Austria, should Philip decline to accept the throne on the terms offered, which required that the realm be held together. Louis XIV accepted on behalf of Philip. The new Bourbon claim on the Spanish throne alarmed all of the powers that feared French expansionism. Austria refused to accept Philip as king of Spain, and went to war against France in 1701. She was supported by several other powers, most notably the United Provinces and Great Britain. Commercial rivalries underlay both Dutch and British belligerency, along with a renewed determination to prevent French domination of the European continent. The War of the Spanish Succession was more than a dynastic quarrel; it was a large-scale conflict of European nation-states fighting over the balance of power in Europe.

In America, the war brought the resumption of French and Indian attacks on New England villages. In the notorious raid on Deerfield, Massachusetts, in 1704, Indians allied with the French killed at least forty-seven townspeople and carried another hundred into captivity. British efforts to secure the safety of the northern colonies by the occupation of Canada ended in failure. The French beat back two efforts to retake Port Royal in 1707. In 1709, colonial authorities abandoned invasion plans when Great Britain failed to make good a promise to provide aid. The following year saw a new offensive, and Port Royal fell to the colonials. In 1711, however, their campaign to take Quebec ended ignominiously when the invasion fleet foundered in the unfamiliar waters of the St. Lawrence River. To the south, a British assault on St. Augustine in Spanish Florida in 1702 had failed to take the city, but a campaign against Spanish missions in West Florida and on the Georgia coast the next year left them in ruins. The raiders, Yamasee Indians recruited by the governor of South Carolina, burned Spanish priests and soldiers at the stake, and seized hundreds of Indian converts, whom they sold to English slave traders. The Spanish and their French allies were unable to mount a successful counterattack. Their joint effort to seize Charleston, South Carolina, in 1706 in an amphibious operation was undone by bad weather and poor coordination.

But while action in North America for the most part was indecisive, Great Britain made some gains elsewhere. Withdrawing from the war in 1713, the British acquired, under the terms of the Treaty of Utrecht,

Gibraltar and Minorca in the Mediterranean. She also obtained from Spain the lucrative *asiento de negros,* a thirty-year monopoly of slave trading rights with the Spanish colonies. In North America, France ceded Nova Scotia, Newfoundland, and Hudson Bay to Britain but kept Cape Breton and Ile St. Jean (Prince Edward Island). In the European settlement, Philip remained on the Spanish throne, but renounced his right to succeed to the throne of France. At the expense of Spain, Austria ultimately gained Naples, Milan, Sardinia, and the Spanish Netherlands.

Louis XIV's military adventures had been very costly to France, in terms of both monetary expense and loss of prestige. In his advice to his great-grandson and successor, the "Sun King" warned, "Do not imitate me in my taste for war." Early in the reign of Louis XV, under the direction of his capable minister Cardinal Fleury, France remained at peace and prospered. But after the cardinal's death, the French government, lacking competent leadership, plunged into conflicts no less disastrous than those the late king regretted.[5]

King George's War 1744–48

Utrecht provided a long truce but no lasting peace. In 1739–43, Great Britain and Spain fought the War of Jenkins's Ear, prompted by disputes over trading rights in Spanish America and named after an English ship captain mutilated by the Spaniards. France was sympathetic to Spain in that conflict, but did not declare war. In Europe, the death of Charles VI of Austria destabilized central Europe. Frederick the Great, king in Prussia, took advantage of the emperor's passing by invading Austrian Silesia in December 1740. When efforts of the powers to negotiate between Frederick and Austria's new empress, Maria Theresa, failed, Europe was plunged into a full-scale war (the War of the Austrian Succession) that aligned Prussia with France and Austria with Great Britain. The issue was not only Prussian occupation of Silesia; it was, once again, the question of containing the power of France, for the French, as one historian notes, now "came closer to dominating Europe than any modern European state prior to Napoleon."[6] Great Britain and France went to war in 1744, as British forces aided the anti-French alliance on the Continent and French and Indian raiders once again struck New England and New York.

In North America this war, named after King George, was marked by a failed French Canadian effort to retake Acadia and by their burning of Saratoga, New York. On the British side, the great French fortress of Louisbourg, at the mouth of the St. Lawrence River, fell to a brilliant siege mounted by colonial militia in 1745. To the consternation of the New Englanders, the Treaty of Aix-la-Chapelle in 1748 returned Louisbourg to France, in exchange for the return of Madras, then a relatively unimportant trading station in India. In North America, King George's War left much of the northern colonial frontier a wasteland of burned-out farmhouses, deserted, overgrown orchards, and abandoned forts, but settled nothing. The boundary lines between British and French territories remained in dispute. France and Britain claimed not only the Ohio River valley but also much of northern New York and New England. The stage was set for a greater conflict, the Seven Years' War, remembered in America as the French and Indian War, a conflict which would end with the destruction of France's North American empire. Its ultimate impact on the British empire, on British colonists, and on Native American peoples would be no less profound.

Origins of the French and Indian War

In 1749, England and France were technically at peace. But at an outpost deep in the North American wilderness, at the site of the future city of Detroit, the French commandant offered to pay a substantial reward for the scalp of a British subject named George Croghan. An Irishman based in Pennsylvania, Croghan had been a thorn in the side of the French for several years. Skilled in Indian diplomacy and fluent in Native American languages, he had established trading posts throughout western territories claimed by France, and had won the support of powerful Indian allies such as the Miami and the Mingos. During the recently concluded war with France, Croghan had helped instigate a Native American uprising against the French in the Ohio country. He had marked his success by sending the scalp of a French trader to Philadelphia.

Croghan kept his own scalp; the bounty was never collected. But the French in Canada moved aggressively to drive English traders from western Pennsylvania and the Ohio valley. A military expedition under the command of Captain Pierre-Joseph Céleron de Blainville marched through the contested territories in 1749, planting metal plates proclaiming French ownership and warning the Indians not to trade with the British. When the Ohio Indians failed to heed Céleron's admonition, a raiding party of pro-French Indians, recruited by Charles Leglande, burned Pickawillany, a pro-English Miami Indian village, in June 1652, murdered its chief, and, in an act of ritual cannibalism that horrified the British and intimidated their Indian clients, ate his body. French troops accompanied by Indian warriors soon thereafter scoured the Ohio valley, killing or imprisoning fifty-two of Croghan's traders. By 1754, Pennsylvania's western Indian trade was defunct and Croghan was bankrupt.

Other, more powerful colonial economic interests also suffered as a result of French Canada's campaign to bar the British from the forests west of the Alleghenies. Land speculators in Pennsylvania and Virginia anticipated great profits from the expansion of British settlement westward. The colony of Virginia claimed the Ohio valley, as did Pennsylvania. Prominent Virginians, including members of George Washington's family, invested in the Ohio Company, a speculative venture to acquire and sell western land. Pennsylvanians, including Benjamin Franklin, poured money into their own competing land companies. French military activities threatened their hopes as well as British territorial claims.

Although the two countries were still at peace, both France and Great Britain had encouraged their respective colonial officials to undertake aggressive action in the west. France's plan was to control trade in the Mississippi and Ohio valleys and, with the help of her Indian allies, confine the British to a narrow strip of land on the Atlantic coast. To that end, the French undertook construction of a chain of forts on western and northern lands claimed by Great Britain. The British were no less determined to claim and ultimately settle the vast interior regions of the continent. In the summer of 1753, the king's cabinet decided that all colonial governors should use force, if necessary, to remove the French from British territory in North America. Since France and Great Britain were both determined to press their claim to the Ohio valley (which included much of western Pennsylvania), were at odds over ownership of much of the St. Lawrence watershed (which extended far into New York), and disagreed about the location of the Nova Scotia boundary, with Britain claiming portions of the adjoining mainland, conflict was unavoidable.

Colonel Washington's Defeat, 1754

In compliance with his instructions from London, Governor Robert Dinwiddie of Virginia sent a delegation led by George Washington, then

a twenty-one-year-old militia officer, to Fort Le Boeuf, a recently constructed French stronghold in northwestern Pennsylvania (near the future
town of Waterford). They presented to the commandant there a letter from
the governor asking that the French withdraw their troops from British
soil. The commandant, after entertaining Washington and his party at
dinner, refused to consider their request. Instead, several months later,
French troops drove away a band of Virginians whom Dinwiddie had sent
to the forks of the Ohio (modern Pittsburgh) with orders to build a fort
to protect British interests in the upper Ohio valley. The French proceeded
to erect their own fort at the strategically critical junction of the Ohio and
Monongahela rivers. They named it Fort Duquesne in honor of the governor of New France.

To reinforce the party at the forks of the Ohio, Dinwiddie dispatched
159 Virginia militiamen assisted by some Iroquois scouts. En route, their
commander died unexpectedly, and Colonel Washington assumed command. Learning that the French had seized the forks, Washington on the
morning of May 28, 1754, mounted a surprise attack on a French detachment at Great Meadows (near the future Uniontown in western Pennsylvania) as they were preparing breakfast The ranking French officer, Ensign
Joseph Coulon de Jumonville, who carried a message demanding that the
Virginians withdraw, was wounded in a volley of gunfire and then killed
by an Indian chief's tomahawk. Nine other French soldiers died in that
engagement. The twenty survivors were taken prisoner and sent to Virginia. The French retaliated, trapping Washington and his men in a makeshift enclosure they called Fort Necessity. On July 4, 1754, Fort Necessity
surrendered. The victorious French officers included in the articles of capitulation signed by Washington an admission that he had illegally "as-
sassinated" Ensign Jumonville. He was then permitted to return to Virginia
with his troops. Washington later claimed he did not know what he was
signing, as he could not read French. After learning of his defeat, the Virginia government appealed to London for help in reoccupying the upper
Ohio valley.

General Braddock's Defeat, 1755

In 1755, the British government was not prepared for resumption
of a full-scale war against France. However, the king's ministers were still
resolved to counter French intrusions into territory claimed by Great

Britain. The duke of Newcastle, head of the British government, declared it essential that they make arrangements to demolish those forts that "have clearly and notoriously been built upon our ground."[7] Since the Virginia militia under Colonel Washington had proved unequal to the task of reclaiming the Ohio valley, London sent a sixty-year-old British general, Edward Braddock of the Coldstream Guards, to Pennsylvania in command of two Irish regiments. To his force of 1,000 professional soldiers, Braddock added 2,500 colonial militia. On July 9, 1755, after cutting its way through forests, Braddock's forward column was within a few miles of Fort Duquesne when it blundered into an unexpected engagement with a small party of French soldiers accompanied by Canadian militia and their Indian allies. As Braddock's men formed a battle line across a narrow road and prepared to confront the French regulars, the Canadians and the Indians fanned out into wooded ravines on both sides of the British. Under cover of the dense foliage, they peppered Braddock's column with gunfire as his advancing troops, blocked by the congestion on the road, milled about and collided with one another. The result: a one-sided slaughter. French and Indian casualties numbered 39; the British lost over 1,000, including Braddock, who died of wounds on July 13.

The general had shown great courage, but his judgment in the battle that claimed his life left much to be desired. By ordering his men to stand and hold their line, rather than take cover, Braddock played into the hands of the enemy. Although some of Braddock's supporters later blamed the defeat on the undisciplined colonials, most authorities have agreed that the battle demonstrated that Great Britain's regular army in 1755 was ill-suited to New World warfare. Although the surviving British force greatly outnumbered the French at Fort Duquesne, Braddock's second in command, Colonel Thomas Dunbar, rather than regrouping and mounting an attack, ordered a retreat. After straggling back to Philadelphia, the once proud army, to the derision of the locals, went into winter quarters in midsummer.

Braddock's defeat was a humiliation of historic proportions. George Washington, serving as a civilian aide to Braddock, summed it up: "We have been most scandalously beaten by a trifling body of men."[8] Of the many reasons given for Braddock's failure, one stands out: lack of intelligence regarding the movements of the enemy. His army should never have been caught unaware on the road to Fort Duquesne. Part of the problem was that Braddock lacked Indian auxiliaries. A contingent of southern Indians promised by the governor of Virginia never arrived. The governor of South Carolina had objected to their service in Pennsylvania. Braddock himself alienated both the Delawares led by Shingas and a group of one hundred Mingos (western Iroquois) recruited by Croghan. One of their chiefs complained that the general treated them "like dogs."[9] All but eight deserted. The lack of Indian assistance in an unfamiliar wilderness placed Braddock's army at a disadvantage.

But that does not entirely explain the disastrous encounter near the French fort. Braddock's officers inexplicably failed to follow standard British army procedures and send out their own scouts. His army thus stumbled blindly into the arms of the enemy. Benjamin Franklin explained Braddock's defeat as follows: "He had too much self-confidence; too high an opinion of the validity of regular troops; too mean a one of both Americans and Indians." But however deficient the general's understanding of the needs of frontier warfare may have been, he was not as blindly self-confident as he appeared, for an old friend related that before he left London, "The General told me that he should never see me more; for he was going with a handful of men to conquer whole nations; and to do so they must cut through unknown woods. He produced a map of the country, saying at the same time . . . we are sent like sacrifices to the altar."[10]

How the British Planned to Win

Before undertaking his march against Fort Duquesne, General Braddock had participated in a series of conferences in London and in the colonies called to devise a strategy for defeating France in North America. That strategy, as it evolved before and after Braddock's death, envisioned a four-pronged attack on French positions in 1755. Those operations were to be carried out by armies composed of colonial militia augmented by regular army troops. In previous Anglo-French wars, operations in North America had been entrusted primarily to colonials. Now they were to receive direct military aid from the mother country. The first of the four land actions against French intruders on the colonial frontier would be commanded by Braddock himself, and was intended to retake the forks of the Ohio. That campaign, as we have noted, ended in disaster. A second offensive would be aimed at Fort Niagara, on the southwest end of Lake

Ontario. Seizure of that stronghold would cut off France's water route to the Ohio valley and the west. A third British force was to strike at Fort St. Frederick (Crown Point) at the southern entrance to Lake Champlain. From Crown Point, the way would be open to invade the St. Lawrence valley and occupy French Canada. A fourth campaign would be mounted from Nova Scotia to lay claim to contested territories on the Atlantic coast. Success of these ventures would be followed by amphibious operations against the fortified French cities on the St. Lawrence River.

Underlying all of these operations was a naval strategy that envisioned a blockade of Canada that would make it impossible for the French to resupply the colony. That aspect of British strategic planning was central to plans to drive the French from the North American continent. New France was not self-sufficient, and could not survive without supplies from Europe. While France had a respectable navy, Great Britain nonetheless enjoyed a very substantial advantage on the high seas. On the eve of the French and Indian War, she "possessed two thirds of the tonnage of the entire world's shipping."[11] Most of her commercial fleet was easily converted to military use. Despite her navy's best efforts, France could not match British sea power.

As we shall see, British execution of the strategy for victory outlined above was marred by errors, accidents, inefficiency, bickering, and ineptness, all contributing to a series of defeats in the early years of the war. But the strategy itself was sound; the British possessed the resources to carry it out; and finally the leadership needed to prevail was found.

How France Planned to Win

French strategy in the North American theater of the war in many respects paralleled Great Britain's. Fully aware of British war plans as a result of the capture of General Braddock's papers, Governor Pierre Vaudreuil and his associates planned an audacious offensive that they hoped would keep the enemy off base and prevent the mustering of the superior numbers and resources the British enjoyed. They believed, to put it briefly, that the best defense is a good offense. Accordingly, Canada's military planners envisioned a four-pronged attack on the British frontiers. The first, executed, as we have seen, in 1754–55, sent French military forces supported by Indian allies into the Ohio valley and culminated in the seizure, fortification, and defense of the forks of the Ohio. The other prongs of invasion struck New York. One, executed in 1756, led to the ejection of the British from Fort Oswego, thereby securing absolute control of Lake Ontario and water access to the west. Another involved the invasion of New York by way of Lake Champlain and culminated in the British defeat at Fort William Henry, on the south end of the lake, in 1757. Indian support was crucial to all of those efforts. The fourth French war zone encompassed the entire frontier. The French believed that Indian raids on British frontier communities from Maine through the Carolinas would help break the British will to resist. The outcome, they hoped, would not only secure possession of Canada and northern New York, but would also establish a permanent French presence in the Ohio and the upper Mississippi valleys, thus linking French Canada and French Louisiana.

In the early years of the conflict, the French war effort in North America was surprisingly successful. But, as we will see, problems with Indian allies and dissension between the regular French army and the colonial forces weakened their later efforts. Most seriously, New France was plagued by shortages of men, materiel, and even food. When Great Britain gained nearly absolute control of the high seas late in the war, France could no longer resupply Canada. But the outcome was by no means inevitable. At each of the major turning points of this war, decisions, good and bad, made by leaders on both sides shaped the course of events. We turn now to a year-by-year review of the war's progress.

British Failures in New York, 1755

Braddock's defeat was not the only British disappointment in 1755. Efforts to deal with French incursions on the northern frontier also ended in failure. Claiming that the entire St. Lawrence watershed belonged to France, the Canadians had built forts in northern New York. Under their sponsorship, Indian raiding parties had struck settlements in both New York and New England, burning farms, killing noncombatants, and taking captives who were sometimes killed, sometimes adopted, but more often sold back to the British colonials via the French. In June 1755 France had dispatched 3,000 regular army troops under the command of Baron Ludwig August Dieskau, a tough and resourceful German serving in the

French army. Although the British captured two ships in the armada conveying Dieskau and the newly appointed governor of New France, over 2,600 of those troops now joined 8,000 Canadian militia and several thousand warriors from over thirty of the Indian nations friendly to the French.[12] New France was prepared.

British preparations were less impressive. The planned offensive against Fort Niagara undertaken by William Shirley, governor of Massachusetts and Braddock's successor as supreme commander, was plagued by desertions and intercolonial bickering. Shirley's army never reached its objective. Had Niagara been taken, the British would have been in a position to block French access to the west. Another army, composed of 2,000 militia and several hundred Mohawk warriors, led by William Johnson, a veteran Indian agent, was supposed to take Fort St. Frederick (Crown Point) in northeastern New York. En route, Johnson's forces on September 8 beat back a fierce assault by the French army led by Dieskau, taking the baron prisoner. Dieskau was surprised by the fighting prowess of Johnson's militiamen. "In the morning," he declared, "they fought like good boys. About noon like men, and in the afternoon like devils."[13] Despite their victory, the militia officers were shaken by the ferocity of Dieskau's attack early in the engagement and disconcerted by reports of the construction of a French fort at Ticonderoga (the French would call it Fort Carillon), commanding the passageway between Lake George and Lake Champlain. They therefore persuaded Johnson to call off plans for an attack on Crown Point. Rather than removing the French intruders as planned, the British now constructed the earth-and-log Fort William Henry on the south end of Lake George. The fort was clearly needed to protect Albany and southern New York from a French invasion.

Rogers's Rangers

After the failure of Johnson's campaign in 1755, the Mohawks and other members of the Iroquois Confederacy, unimpressed by British prospects, refused to provide any further aid. They would not reverse that decision until 1759, when it became apparent that the French would lose. To fill the gap left by the loss of Iroquois scouts, colonial militia leaders organized ranger units. The best-known, commanded by the New Hampshire militia captain Robert Rogers, was mobilized during the New York campaign in 1755. Rogers was also given responsibility for training other units. Captain Rogers's orders, as he related them, were not only to gather intelligence but also "to distress the French and their allies, by sacking, burning, and destroying their houses, barns, barracks, canoes, bateaux, etc.," orders he carried out with legendary zeal.[14] Frontier warfare had long been brutal and inhumane. The British sometimes claimed moral superiority to the French, but the secretary to New York's royal governor spoke for many when he urged that colonial soldiers "deal exactly with them [the French] as they do by us, destroy and scalp as they do. They set their Indians to scalping our poor defenseless inhabitants, in this the necessity pleads an excuse for following so inhuman an example."[15] The scalping knife was part of the standard equipment of Rogers's Rangers, for the captain taught colonial farm boys how to fight Indian-style. Rogers became a legendary figure, celebrated in plays, novels, and histories for the next two centuries. Those who romanticized Rogers and his rangers overlooked both his high casualty rate and his ruthlessness, as revealed in his massacre of 200 Indians at the village of St. Francis on October 5, 1759. Rogers justified his killing of noncombatants (a violation of General Jeffrey Amherst's orders) by claiming, "We found in the town hanging on the poles over their doors, &c about 600 scalps, mostly English."[16]

The Exile of the Acadians

The campaign to assert territorial claims in Nova Scotia (acquired from France at the end of Queen Anne's War in 1713 but still the subject of boundary disputes) had provided Britain's only victory in North America in 1755. In June, two French forts, Beausejour and Gaspereau, situated on the isthmus of Chignecto connecting Nova Scotia to the mainland, surrendered to Colonel Robert Monckton, commander of an army composed of 2,000 New England militiamen and 270 British soldiers from the Halifax garrison. Despite the ejection of French forces, the British nonetheless felt insecure, for much of the local population, known as Acadians, encouraged by Catholic clergy and French officials, refused to swear an oath of allegiance to the British king that would obligate them to bear arms. The local British authorities, in an act that remains notorious to this day, therefore took advantage of the presence of Monckton's army to order the expulsion of those who had not taken the oath. Half of the local Acadian population was deported. Some were transported to other British colonies. Others escaped to Canada or to France. A few made their way to French Louisiana. Some remained in the area and joined the Micmac Indians in terrorizing the new British settlement at Halifax. Distrusted by both the English and the French, the Acadians fared poorly under both.

The French Counterattack, 1756–57

Following the collapse of the British offensive against Fort Duquesne, the French made good use of that base to consolidate their alliance with the Indian nations of the upper Ohio valley and use them in waging war against British frontier settlements. Within a year Indian raiders, numbering at least 2,000 in all, had struck scores of frontier settlements not only in Pennsylvania but also in Maryland, Virginia, and the Carolinas, killing or capturing around 3,000 British settlers. Dieskau's replacement, Louis Joseph, marquis de Montcalm, wrote from Quebec to his wife in France, "The savages have made great havoc in Pennsylvania and Virginia, and carried off, according to their custom, men, women, and children." George Washington, commanding Virginia's frontier militia, declared, "Every day we have accounts of cruelties and barbarities that are shocking to human nature. It is not possible to conceive the situation and danger of this miserable country. Such numbers of French and Indians are all around that no roads are safe."[17] Not only isolated farms were put to the torch; in August 1756, Fort Granville, on the Juniata River in Pennsylvania, fell to a Delaware Indian raiding party, forcing a wholesale British evacuation of the region. Soon French and Indian raiders struck within seventy miles of Philadelphia. At Fort Duquesne (modern Pittsburgh) it is said that 500 scalps, mostly from Pennsylvanians killed by raiders, hung from scalp poles.

In March 1756, the British government, provoked by the French seizure of Minorca in the Mediterranean, finally acknowledged the existence of hostilities by declaring war on France. The Seven Years' War saw a new alignment of powers. Austria, previously a British ally, now made common cause with France. Prussia, hitherto an ally of France, was now supported by Great Britain in the land war in Europe. The conflict that had begun in the backwoods of Pennsylvania soon expanded to encompass the entire globe. Worldwide, the war would claim a million lives. Most of the dead fell on the battlefields of Europe.

The French offensive in North America was not limited to the west. In March 1756, a small French and Indian force struck Fort Bull, a minor outpost on the road to Oswego, the major British fort commanding the approaches to Lake Ontario. The raiders killed or took prisoner the members of the garrison, and then destroyed a large cache of gunpowder and supplies badly needed at Oswego. The following summer, a much larger French force, commanded by Montcalm, besieged Oswego itself. The forts at Oswego were in disrepair and the garrison lacked adequate supplies. During the previous year, over half of the British stationed there had died of hunger, exposure, or disease. Not only were many of the soldiers forced to sleep on the ground, but there was little food to be had. One of the officers who survived testified that "had the poor fellows lived, they must have eaten one another."[18] Reinforcements dispatched to Oswego could not save it from the French invaders. After a short and dispirited defense, in which the British commander was killed, the outnumbered British at Fort Oswego surrendered. The French leveled the fort to the ground and sent nearly 1,700 prisoners to Canada. In one of the many atrocities of this war, Montcalm failed to prevent his Indian allies from scalping and killing a number of wounded British captives.

The "Massacre" at Fort William Henry, 1757

Hostilities on the northern frontier resumed the following summer. In 1757, the French remained dominant. A British attempt, under the new supreme commander, John Campbell, Lord Loudoun, to invade Canada was poorly prepared, plagued by bad weather and woefully poor intelligence, and was abandoned before it really got underway. Benjamin Franklin declared Loudoun's abortive campaign "frivolous, expensive, and disgraceful to our Nation beyond Conception."[19] The recently appointed governor of New France, the marquis Pierre de Vaudreuil, was determined to eliminate the British threat before a new invasion could be mounted. In pursuit of the objective, he ordered his army to seize Fort William Henry. After earlier efforts failed to breech the fort's formidable defenses, Montcalm, commanding a powerful invasion force of 8,000 men, including nearly 2,000 warriors from thirty-three Indian nations, some from as far away as Illinois, laid siege on August 2, 1757. After a week of gallant resistance, the British garrison surrendered. Montcalm, moved by the valor of his adversary, ordered that the British should be given full military honors, which meant they would not be made prisoners of war, but would be allowed to keep their arms, withdraw with flags flying, and return to their homes, with the understanding that they would not fight against France for at least eighteen months.

Montcalm's Indian allies were angered and disappointed by the general's generosity. They believed that a promise had been broken. The French had led them to expect plunder, scalps, and captives. Although Montcalm asked the Indian leaders to respect the terms of the surrender, some could not, or would not, restrain their warriors. The night before the evacuation of the British, Indians within the fort killed some of the wounded. The next day, Indians clamoring for plunder stole the personal possessions of the defeated soldiers, grabbing the backpacks of common soldiers and rifling through their contents, and tearing open the baggage of officers. The French troops did nothing to stop them, but advised the British not to resist. Some of the warriors next assaulted the British column, which included women and children, as it marched away from Fort William Henry. They seized and scalped some of the soldiers, but in most cases took captives, to serve as slaves or sell for ransom. Montcalm promptly intervened to secure the release of several hundred of those captives, but a number of Indians ignored his pleas. New France's governor later rescued most of those captives, buying their freedom from the Indians. Some, however, were killed by their captors.

Eyewitness accounts disagree as to the role of other French officers. It appears that while some intervened to protect the English, others did not. The killings were brief, and were the work of only a few of the 1,600 Indians still on the scene. Most of the 2,500 British at Fort William Henry escaped unscathed. While accounts vary, it appears that sixty-nine died at the hands of the Indians at Fort William Henry. Another 200 or so were taken away as captives. The Fort William Henry Massacre, as it came to be known, was a blot on the honor of France and on the reputation of Montcalm, who twice had been unable to control his Indian allies. But Indian savagery and French complicity in the atrocity were both greatly exaggerated as the British retold the story. Lurid accounts of the killings after the surrender came to be an important part of the Anglo-American folklore of the frontier. Stories of the massacre were used to justify the demonization of both the French and the Indians.[20]

Soon after the altercation with Montcalm over their right to captives, most of his Indian allies left Fort William Henry. The French forces now lacked adequate Indian support. Defying his orders from Governor Vaudreuil, which directed that he proceed to take Fort Edward to the south, the general ended his campaign and marched his men back to Canada. Upon his return, Montcalm and Vaudreuil quarreled over military strategy, with the governor demanding that the offensive in northern New York and the Ohio country be maintained, and the general warning that priority must now be given to the defense of Quebec and Montreal. Montcalm feared a British invasion. His anxiety was not misplaced.

The Tide Turns, 1758

At the close of 1757, a new government in London, headed by the able and aggressive commoner William Pitt, changed the direction of British strategy in the Seven Years' War. The major emphasis would no longer be on land victories in Europe, where the king's favorite son, the duke of Cumberland, in command of allied troops had just suffered a crushing defeat, but on attacking France's overseas possessions throughout the world. Pitt was not satisfied with simply containing French aggression on the frontier; he was determined to drive the French from the North American continent. He was therefore prepared to pour unprecedented resources into the American theater of war. Pitt's commitment of 24,000 British troops, along with his demand that the colonial governors raise 25,000 provincials to join them in crushing the French, transformed the conflict. Those quotas were never actually met, but sufficient forces were soon available to support offensives against all of France's major outposts. For the campaigns of 1758, Pitt's officers in North America commanded over 50,000 men, most of them in their twenties. That was a number equivalent to two-thirds of the entire French population on the Continent. To defend New France, Montcalm could muster half as many men only by conscripting into the militia every able-bodied male between the ages of fifteen and sixty.

Even so, the beginning of the British offensive in 1758 was inauspicious. General James Abercromby, Loudoun's replacement as military commander, despite a four-to-one advantage in manpower, bungled an assault on Fort Carillon (Ticonderoga) that was intended to set the stage for an invasion of Canada via Lake Champlain. Montcalm, the defender, did not have the resources needed to protect the fort from a well-thought-out offensive. But Abercromby foolishly mounted a frontal assault, inspired by a false rumor that Montcalm would soon be joined by a huge detachment of French soldiers. A fussy and inept commander called "Granny" (behind his back) by his men, the general was unnerved by those imaginary French reinforcements. Without first deploying his artillery or obtaining a thorough and accurate account of the fort's defenses, on July 8 he hurled his men against a barrier of fallen and tangled trees that Montcalm had hastily erected around the approaches to the fort. The sharpened branches protruding from that defensive barrier (called an *abattis*) have been described as the eighteenth-century equivalent of barbed or concertina wire. One soldier who took cover behind a tree stump later described the effect of French fire from the fort on the troops as they struggled to get through the *abattis*: "I could hear the men screaming and see them dying all around me. I lay there some time. A man could not stand erect without being hit, any more than he could stand out in a shower, without having drops of rain fall upon him, for the balls came in handfuls."[21] After six waves had sustained casualties estimated at around 10 percent of his army, General Abercromby, who had remained in the rear until the evening and did not see much of the battle, ordered a retreat to Fort Edward. Poor intelligence and bad judgment had deprived the British of what should have been an easy victory. Abercromby did not know enough about the nature of French defenses or about their weaknesses at Fort Carillon to frame a practical plan of attack. An artillery bombardment was essential to clear the way into the fort. Montcalm was astounded by Abercromby's retreat, for the British forces still greatly outnumbered his own.

After Abercromby's failure, the tide turned as more capable commanders made better use of the ample resources now available for the invasion of Canada. At the entrance to the St. Lawrence River, a difficult and sometimes problematic amphibious assault on the great French bastion at Louisbourg ended in a British victory on July 26. The victorious general, Jeffrey Amherst, imposed a hard peace. His troops killed and scalped Indians who had aided the French. Amherst sent the Louisbourg garrison soldiers who survived the siege as war prisoners to England. Civilians in the region (on Cape Breton and Prince Edward islands) he deported to France, declaring their landed property forfeit. His terms, harsh if judged by the standards and conventions of European warfare, reflected British outrage over the "massacre" at Fort

William Henry. One recent historian suggests they also served the interests of British land speculators.[22]

A month after the fall of Louisbourg, forces led by Colonel John Bradstreet took Fort Frontenac in Canada, on the northeastern shore of Lake Ontario. Bradstreet, a colonial militia officer of English and French ancestry who had been born in Nova Scotia, overcame the opposition of more cautious British officers to carry out an audacious attack that ended in winning total control of the strategically critical water route to the west. Resupply and reinforcement of the French outposts in the west were now virtually impossible. In the Ohio country, an army under the command of Brigadier General John Forbes drove the defenders from Fort Duquesne late in November. The forks of the Ohio were once again in British hands.

Forbes's offensive had been greatly assisted by the diplomatic efforts of men such as Frederick Post and George Croghan, who very skillfully persuaded many of the Delaware, Shawnee, and Mingo tribesmen previously loyal to France that support of the French war effort was no longer in their interest. Since the French now had great difficulty in supplying Indian allies with the goods they needed and expected, the warnings of the forest diplomats carried great weight. With the western Indians finally inclined to neutrality, France's position in the Ohio valley was now in great jeopardy. Even so, the negotiations were difficult, for, as Post noted, the Indians remained "afraid that the English will take their land."[23] To detach the western Indians from the French, the negotiators promised that the British in victory would respect their territorial rights. That promise, as we shall see, was not kept.

The War in 1759: The Fall of Quebec

British historians often call 1759 the *annus mirabilis*, the "wonderful year." In India, British arms prevailed, and France's colonial aspirations on the subcontinent were shattered. In the West Indies, England seized the French island of Guadeloupe. In Europe, in the battle of Quiberon Bay in Brittany, the British destroyed much of France's navy, crippling her capacity to resupply Canada and other overseas possessions. In North America, the decision of the League of the Iroquois to commit warriors to the British cause signaled the beginning of the end of French power. Early in the year, Six Nations' chiefs, impressed by the fall of Fort

Duquesne and hoping, with the aid of the victors, to regain their former dominant position in the west, told Sir William Johnson that they were now "ready to join and revenge your Blood and ours upon the French."[24] On July 9, Fort Niagara, which commanded the strait between lakes Ontario and Erie, fell to a British force commanded, after the accidental death of Brigadier General John Prideaux, by Johnson. The loss of Niagara completely severed New France's water access to the west. In that engagement 3,000 British and colonial troops were supported by 1,000 Iroquois warriors, who used their influence to persuade most of the Indians defending the French garrison to declare their neutrality and withdraw from the fight.

The greatest engagement of the year, and of the war, was the campaign against Quebec, a naval operation supported by over 140 ships that transported 9,000 troops up the St. Lawrence River in June. Montcalm, supported by 15,000 French and Canadian soldiers and 1,000 Indian auxiliaries, mostly from the Catholic missions, had prepared a formidable defense. He was inadvertently assisted in that endeavor by General Jeffrey Amherst, the new British supreme commander in North America, whose campaigns against the French forts at Crown Point and Ticonderoga, although successful, fell behind schedule. Amherst's failure to invade Canada in a timely manner weakened the Quebec campaign by giving Montcalm an opportunity to gather his forces.

The British commander at Quebec, Brigadier General James Wolfe, subjected the city to a withering artillery bombardment and ravaged the surrounding countryside. Although his troops were outnumbered by Montcalm's army, Wolfe, scornful of both the Canadian and the British colonial militias, was convinced that his regular army men could carry the day. But he was frustrated by Montcalm's tactics. "The enemy," Wolfe reported, "puts nothing to risk . . . my antagonist has wisely shut himself up in inaccessible entrenchments, so that I can't get at him, without spilling a torrent of blood, and that perhaps to little purpose. The Marquis de Montcalm is at the head of a great number of bad soldiers, and I am at the head of a small number of good ones, but the wary old fellow avoids an action."[25]

Hoping to force Montcalm to engage his army, Wolfe ordered his troops to terrorize the local population. The invaders burned, looted, and slaughtered throughout August. They destroyed at least 1,400 farms. Some estimates claim 4,000 were put to the torch.[26] The civilian casualties cannot be estimated, but the killings were sometimes indiscriminate. Wolfe had ordered his men to spare women and children, and scalp only Indians and Frenchmen in Indian garb, but those restrictions were not always observed. To cite one particularly horrendous example, on August 23 "a detachment of the 23rd regulars captured, killed and scalped a priest and thirty of his parishioners at Ste. Anne."[27]

Montcalm did not take the bait. Wolfe could not lure the French and Canadian forces onto the open field, nor could he find an adequate beachhead on the riverfront that would enable him to break through Quebec's defenses. An attempted landing at Montmorency in midsummer had led to a costly British defeat as Wolfe's men were subjected to withering French fire from the cliffs above. For over two months Montcalm held the city, despite intensified British shelling that leveled most of the buildings within its confines. Finally, on September 13, in one of the most audacious actions in military history, Wolfe and his men landed above the city and, carrying two artillery pieces, scaled a cliff, 150 feet high, at Anse de Foulon on the St. Lawrence. Overcoming a small French guard, they were now on the Plains of Abraham, near the walls of Quebec. Montcalm, underestimating the strength of Wolfe's force, attacked without waiting for the reinforcements that might have turned the tide of battle. The struggle on the Plains of Abraham was over in half an hour. Both generals were among the 1,200 casualties. Wolfe died on the field. Montcalm succumbed to his wounds a day later. His army had been cut to pieces by the invaders. The city surrendered on September 18.

1760–63: The End of the War

In the spring of 1760, the chevalier Francois de Levis attempted the recapture of Quebec, but failed. That fall, the British laid siege to Montreal. Plagued by massive desertions of both French and Canadian troops, no longer assisted by Indian allies, and with no real hope of help from France, Governor Vaudreuil surrendered Canada to the invaders on September 8, 1760. Elsewhere, the war continued for two more years. The British occupied additional islands in the French Caribbean. When Spain belatedly entered the war on the side of France, Great Britain responded by seizing Havana and Manila.

The expenses of war were burdensome, however, so in 1762 Great Britain sought a negotiated peace. In the Peace of Paris of 1763, France regained some Caribbean sugar islands that had been seized by the British during the war. But she abandoned her colonial claims in India and gave up all of Canada, with the exception of two small islands, St. Pierre and Miquelon, off the coast of Newfoundland. The British reoccupied Minorca and took Florida from Spain. Spain had earlier received title to French Louisiana, which then included a vast and largely unexplored region between the Mississippi River and the Rocky Mountains.

Great Britain was now clearly the dominant colonial power in North America. She would face new challenges from France in the years to come. The Peace of Paris offered no permanent settlement of the Anglo-French world power struggle. But France's aspirations to restore her former glory were not Britain's main problem in the years immediately after the war. As we shall see, the British triumph on the Plains of Abraham would lead, paradoxically, to severe problems both with her American colonies and with the Native American peoples who had played so crucial a role in the great war for empire.

Notes

1. Reuben Gold Thwaites, ed., *Early Western Travels 1748–1846*, 32 vols. (Cleveland: Arthur H. Clark, 1904), 1:206–7.

2. Benjamin Church, *The History of the Eastern Expeditions of 1689, 1690, 1692, and 1704, Against the Indians and the French* (Boston: J.K. Wiggin and W.P. Lunt, 1867), 111–12.

3. Quoted in Alan Taylor, *American Colonies* (New York: Viking, 2001), 290.

4. Noel St. John Williams, *Redcoats Along the Hudson: The Struggle for North America, 1754–63* (London: Brassey's, 1998), 8.

5. Quoted in Frank W. Brecher, *Losing a Continent: France's North American Policy, 1753–1763* (Westport, CT: Greenwood Press, 1998), 9.

6. Jeremy Black, *Eighteenth Century Europe*, 2nd ed. (New York: St. Martin's Press, 1999), 336.

7. Quoted in Lawrence Henry Gipson, "A French Project for Victory Short of a Declaration of War, 1755," *Canadian Historical Review* 26 (1945): 362.

8. Quoted in Howard Peckham, *The Colonial Wars, 1689–1762* (Chicago: University of Chicago Press, 1964), 147.

9. Quoted in Nicholas B. Wainwright, *George Croghan: Wilderness Diplomat* (Chapel Hill: University of North Carolina Press, 1959), 94.

10. Quoted in Francis B. Parkman, *Montcalm and Wolfe* (New York: Da Capo Press, 1995), 111–12.

11. Walter L. Dorn, *Competition for Empire, 1740–1763* (New York: Harper, 1963), 16.

12. Ian K. Steele, *Betrayals: Fort William Henry and the "Massacre"* (New York: Oxford University Press, 1990), 42–43.

13. Quoted in Williams, *Redcoats Along the Hudson*, 85.

14. Robert Rogers, *Rogers' Journals* (New York: Corinth Books, 1966), 11.

15. John Sullivan, ed., *The Papers of Sir William Johnson,* 14 vols. (Albany: State University of New York, 1921–65), 11:172–73.

16. Rogers, *Journals,* 111.

17. Quoted in Parkman, *Montcalm and Wolfe*, 193, 213.

18. Ibid., 231.

19. Peckham, *Colonial Wars,* 161.

20. Steele, *Betrayals,* 109–86.

21. Quoted in Fred Anderson, *Crucible of War: The Seven Years' War and the Fate of Empire in British North America* (New York: Alfred A. Knopf, 2000), 244.

22. Ibid., 255.

23. Quoted in ibid., 280.

24. E.B. O'Callaghan and B. Fernow, eds. *Documents Relative to the Colonial History of the State of New York,* 15 vols. (Albany, N.Y.: Weed and Parsons, 1853–87), 7:386.

25. Williams, *Redcoats Along the Hudson,* 175.

26. W.J. Eccles, *Essays on New France* (Toronto: Oxford University Press, 1987), 22.

27. Anderson, *Crucible of War,* 788.

CHAPTER 2

NATIVE AMERICANS AND EUROPEAN INTRUDERS:
AN ONGOING CRISIS

On the eve of the French and Indian War, the interior regions of eastern North America were still occupied almost exclusively by Native Americans. Although the first permanent English and French colonies had been founded nearly a century and a half earlier, and Spanish Florida some years before that, white occupation for the most part was still confined to the eastern and southern coastal regions. Only a small handful of European traders and missionaries had penetrated the vast regions beyond the Allegheny and Appalachian mountain barriers. The British populated the Atlantic seaboard from Maine through Georgia. Spain still controlled Florida. French colonization was centered in the St. Lawrence valley of Canada, but included small settlements on the Gulf of Mexico and some trading posts on the Mississippi.

Since none of the European powers had a substantial presence in the interior, relations with the Indian nations of the Ohio valley, the Mississippi valley, and the Great Lakes region were of crucial importance in their bids to control the continent. To understand the choices made by Native American peoples during the French and Indian War, one must first understand the effects of European colonialism on their lives. Contact with the colonizers changed the Indians' world, in some cases radically. Their responses to their new circumstances were varied, but all were affected, even those who lived hundreds of miles from the nearest English or French settlement. Indian interactions with Europeans were complex, sometimes profitable and rewarding for both parties, but often destructive. While recognizing that Native Americans were not all alike and did not all respond to the European presence in the same way, let us examine the world that emerged from the ongoing encounters of Indians and colonizers in North America.

Disease and Depopulation

When Christopher Columbus landed on an island not far from Florida in 1492, the human inhabitants of North America probably numbered between 5 and 10 million. Within a century of first contact, the Indian populations in the various regions of the Americas shrank by at least 90 percent.[1] Early English accounts of exploration and settlement tell a grim story. The chronicler of an expedition to North Carolina in 1586 reported: "The people began to die very fast . . . the disease [was] so strange, that they neither knew what it was, nor how to cure it, the like by report of the oldest men in the country never happened before, time out of mind."[2] In 1632 a trader in New England wrote of finding deserted Indian villages filled with dead bodies lying on the ground or rotting in their wigwams. "In this place where many inhabited, there hath been but one left alive, to tell what became of the rest, the living being (as it seems) not able to bury the dead, they were left for crows, kites, and vermin to play upon. And the bones and skulls upon the several places of their habitation, made such a spectacle . . . that as I traveled in that forest . . . it seemed to me a new found Golgatha." [3]

Indians often thought that the Europeans killed them through witchcraft. In New France (Canada) missionary priests were sometimes put to death by Indians who believed they had used their powers to spread death through their villages. And Europeans, ignorant of the scientific causes of disease, suspected that God was inflicting epidemics on the Indians to punish them for their sins. But the real reason for the high mortality was that Native American populations, isolated from other human groups since their migration into the continent at least 15,000 years earlier, lacked immunity to the germs and viruses carried by the newcomers. Europeans, having been exposed to those microorganisms for many centuries, were far less vulnerable. Among the deadly diseases that ravaged Indian villages were smallpox, influenza, bubonic plague, pneumonia, tuberculosis, yellow fever, diphtheria, and measles. The epidemics began with the first contacts with European sailors and fishermen in the early sixteenth century and continued for several centuries. The first infections often killed half or more of the inhabitants of villages visited by Europeans. It is believed trade goods carried by Indians from the coast may have spread disease to the Indians in remote interior regions who had never seen Europeans.

The terrible effects of such massive losses of population on Indian life are hard to imagine, but must be taken into account in order to understand later Indian relationships with whites. To those who survived, it seemed as if the world had nearly ended. Indian shamans could no longer heal the sick. Often they succumbed themselves, plunging their communities into a spiritual crisis. The very young and the very old were usually the first to die. Their deaths deprived the living of both their past and much of their future. In 1645 a New England chief, mourning the loss of the elders, lamented, "The wise men [who] in a grave manner taught the people knowledge . . . are dead, and their wisdom is buried with them. . . ."[4] Out of the horrors of plague and epidemic, Indians emerged wary of whites yet, for reasons we shall now investigate, increasingly dependent upon them.

Trade: A Necessity and a Danger

When the Italian explorer Giovanni da Verrazano, sailing in the service of the king of France, visited the Atlantic coast of New England in 1524 (almost two and a half centuries before the French and Indian War), he was astounded to discover that the Indians there were already familiar with European trade goods, and knew what they wanted and what they would pay. Verrazano and his crew did a brisk trade, exchanging various metal and glass items for furs. Having previously encountered European sailors, the Indians were sometimes fearful and sometimes contemptuous; in Maine, Verrazano's men were mooned by jeering Indians who gathered offshore. But everywhere, Verrazano discovered, Indians wanted to trade, even if some insisted that goods be exchanged by lowering and raising them in baskets from a high cliff, in order to avoid direct contact. After the English and French colonies were established in the following century, trade between Indians and colonists became an essential part of the lives of both groups.

Shortly after the end of the French and Indian War, British General Thomas Gage explained, in a letter to Lord Hillsborough, "Our Manufactures are as much desired by the Indians, as their Peltry [fur] is sought for by us; what was originally deemed a Superfluity or a Luxury to the

Natives is now become a Necessary; they are disused to the Bow, and can neither hunt nor make war, without Fire-Arms, Powder and Lead. The British Provinces only can supply them with their Necessaries, which they know, and for their own Sakes they would protect the trade, which they actually do now."[5] To understand the choices various Indian nations made during the French and Indian War, remember General Gage's observation.

The appeal of European trade goods to Indian peoples is easily understood. But the explanation for their demand for those commodities is not that Indians were desperately poor without them. While Native Americans in 1492 were still living in a Stone Age economy, their way of life was not as crude or as lacking in comfort as many have imagined. Indian peoples were generally well nourished and reasonably healthy. In the early years of their contact with Native Americans, European explorers and settlers marveled at the natural abundance they enjoyed. Game was plentiful. Indians hunted wildfowl, deer, moose, and caribou, as well as bison, which then ranged as far east as New York. (The last buffalo east of the Mississippi was shot by a white hunter in Kentucky in 1792.) As for fish, a French Jesuit missionary writing from the St. Lawrence valley of Canada in 1636 reported that the river was "full of Sturgeon, Salmon, Shad, Pike, flounder, whitefish, carp of different kinds. . . . There are some lakes where one could live on fish summer and winter. This last summer some of our French caught Pike there three or four feet long, Sturgeon of four or five feet, and other fish in abundance."[6]

To that natural bounty Indians added the produce of their cultivated fields. With the exception of a few northern tribes who were exclusively hunter-gatherers, most Indian peoples east of the Mississippi—including some in Canada—had developed a highly successful horticulture that produced surpluses of the basic crops, corn, beans, and squash. Women tilled the fields. Men provided animal protein by hunting and fishing. Indian horticultural techniques minimized soil erosion. As hunters, they generally killed only as much game as they could use. (There were some exceptions, such as the practice often used to hunt buffalo on the Great Plains which involved driving them over cliffs.) Native Americans observed rituals to placate the spirits of those animals whose lives they took and to assure both their rebirth and their continued favor. The impact on the environment of the traditional Native American horticultural and hunting economy was minimal, not because of taboos against killing animals, but because subsistence societies with limited trade had little need or use for surpluses that could not be consumed locally.[7] Although Europeans generally scorned Indians as an improvident people who did not value enterprise or wealth, some early observers reported that Native Americans were generally taller and healthier than most Europeans, a conclusion that has been confirmed by some recent archaeological discoveries.[8] They were seldom hungry, and because their societies emphasized sharing and discouraged selfishness, no one went without the basic necessities of life and no one was wealthy. But bear in mind that by modern standards Indian life was devoid of the comforts, amenities, and privacy we take for granted. One suspects that most of their twenty-first-century New Age admirers would have a very hard time adjusting to life in a real sixteenth-century Indian village.

The technology that supported the Native American economy was fairly simple. Though pounded copper or, rarely, gold might be used in jewelry, Indians had not developed metallurgy. Their ax blades, spear points, arrowheads, and knives were all made of stone. Woven baskets or fired pottery provided cooking vessels and storage containers. East of the Mississippi, Indians did not possess woven textiles, but wore skins and hides. They brought great skill and artistry to the making of their clothing, weapons, pots, baskets, and mats. The birch bark canoe, lightweight and mobile, to cite one example of their achievements, was a truly remarkable invention. Indian wigwams and longhouses, constructed of wood and woven mats, were not only remarkably easy to construct and transport, but were warmer in winter than the drafty houses European colonists erected in the American wilderness. Although they offered no privacy and little personal space, they were well suited to the needs of a communal, subsistence economy.

Some European thinkers envied the Indians, seeing in their simple, egalitarian way of life a reflection of a lost "Golden Age." But Native Americans were even more envious of European technology, and were astounded by the trade goods offered to them by the newcomers. In both hunting and warfare, metal axes, swords, spear points, and arrowheads were far more efficient in killing than their stone counterparts. To clear a field or skin a carcass, an implement of iron had great advantage over one of wood and stone. An iron or copper cooking pot was far easier to use and transport than a woven basket or pottery vessel. European cloth was of lighter weight than skins or furs, and came in colors unlike anything they had ever seen. Possession of those goods could make life easier. Much of the

Indian interest in European trade was inspired by the very human desire to enjoy a higher standard of living.

But that is not the whole story. Possession of European goods also brought power and prestige. Indeed, in order to be secure from Indian rivals and enemies, access to European weaponry was soon a necessity. A chief whose warriors were armed with metal weapons was in a far stronger position than a chief whose warriors had to rely on stone-tipped arrowheads and stone battle-axes. The tribe that possessed guns, gunpowder, and shot was better equipped for war than one that did not. Hence, from the earliest years of colonization, Native American peoples vied with one another for access to European weaponry. While some colonies tried to restrict the Indians' access to guns, there were always traders willing and able to meet their needs. By the late seventeenth century, Indian wars were waged with European weaponry.

The desire for trade goods as a means of attaining power was not limited to instruments of war. Many Indians believed that glass and metal goods were of supernatural origin. An English expedition to North Carolina in 1584 traded a shiny tin plate to a local chief who believed that if he wore it around his neck, it would defend him from his enemies' arrows. Other Indians, shown English magnets, a telescope, a mirror, and a gun, declared that those miraculous objects must have been made by gods. In the early years of contact, Indians throughout North America commonly broke up metal pots and wore the pieces as magical amulets. The Indian demand for glass beads of certain colors and for other ornamental objects, such as mirrors, combs, and rings, must be understood, at least in part, in terms of a quest for spiritual empowerment. Although that particular understanding of European trade goods had faded by the time of the French and Indian War, a residual belief in their exceptional nature lingered.

In the short run, trade with Europeans did enhance the material well-being of those Native American peoples fortunate enough to establish favorable connections with English, Dutch, or French traders. But soon that trade proved harmful to Indian well-being. The main trade goods Europeans wanted from Indians were animal furs and hides. To gain and keep European trade partners, Indians began killing furbearing animals in such numbers that in some areas beaver (a main source of furs and hides for trade) were wiped out. In 1705, Robert Beverley, governor of Virginia, reported that the Indians were killing deer by the thousands: "They make all this Slaughter only for the Sake of the Skins, leaving the Carcasses to perish in the Woods." Beaver and some smaller furbearing animals had virtually disappeared from New England and New York by 1700. The deer population was also severely depleted. The seventeenth-century Indian fur trade, combined with an ongoing white determination to exterminate predators such as wolves, devastated North America's animal population. Early in the nineteenth century, Timothy Dwight found that in New England there were "hardly any wild animals remaining besides a few small species of no consequence."[9]

Trade with Europeans not only altered Native American relationships with the animal world; it also had an enormous impact on their daily lives. One trade commodity was particularly destructive of Indian well-being. Prior to colonization the people of eastern North America used no alcoholic beverages. Soon after first contact, rum and brandy were in great demand. For reasons not fully understood, the liquor trade had a devastating effect on Native Americans. On the eve of the French and Indian War, a French Jesuit missionary reported that Indians, normally "the gentlest and most tractable of men, become, when intoxicated, madmen and wild beasts. They fall upon one another, stab with their knives, and tear one another. Many have lost ears and some a portion of their noses in these tragic encounters."[10] Comparable reports came from every frontier region and every Indian community from the seventeenth century onward. Traders commonly related that after trading liquor to their Indian clients for pelts, they would often find the bodies of Indian men and women along the trail in the morning, dead of alcohol poisoning or killed by crazed fellow drinkers. French and English missionaries and government officials often called for regulation or prohibition of the liquor trade, as did tribal leaders. Their efforts were almost always unsuccessful. Unscrupulous white traders used liquor to defraud their Indian suppliers, as did land companies and even some colonial diplomats.

Trade with Europeans undermined Native American societies in other ways. While European trade goods in the early years were regarded as either military necessities (in the case of weapons) or as prestigious luxury items, within a generation or so Indians became totally dependent on imports. They ceased hunting with bows and arrows. They stopped producing their own pottery. As game disappeared, they became dependent on Europeans for some of their food, purchasing European domesticated animals. And in many cases, they lost the skills needed to resume their own way of life. In 1761 British Indian agent John Stuart reported, "A modern Indian cannot subsist without Europeans and would handle a flint ax or any other rude utensil used by his ancestors very awkwardly, so what was only Conveniency at first now becomes Necessity."[11] Indians were thus in an extremely vulnerable position, since they could neither manufacture the new-style European goods they now depended upon nor restore their own earlier way of life. No longer self-sufficient, Indians in the new colonial economy were now suppliers of raw materials for others, and lacked real economic clout. The profits of the fur trade went to the Europeans. The Indians were victims of uneven exchanges.

The impact of trade on the Native American way of life was far-reaching. In terms of the material aspects of their culture, by the eighteenth century Indians generally wore shirts, vests, scarves, and turbans bought from traders along with traditional breechclouts and leggings. They often lived in European-style log cabins, with a few sticks of furniture and some crockery purchased from traders. A French or British trader was generally in residence even in the more remote Indian villages, and sometimes a missionary as well. Indian men no longer hunted nearby to provide for their families and kin, but were often gone for months at a time in search of the furs or skins to exchange for the trade goods their people now could not live without. They were armed with rifles, but so great was their dependence on Europeans that Indians could neither repair guns nor manufacture powder and shot.

At home, the absence of game led to food shortages. The women of the villages had to work far harder to raise more crops to make up for that loss. Everyone worked harder now. Men and women alike had less leisure and, despite the new manufactured goods they possessed, were not very well-off. Whereas European travelers had once idealized Indian villages as places where a simple people close to nature enjoyed natural abundance, reports now generally spoke of poverty, drunkenness, and squalor. In the early eighteenth century Indian religious prophets deplored the loss of communal values, and warned that the Great Spirit was punishing Indians because they had become as selfish and materialistic as the Europeans.

Indian Warfare

Warfare had long been an important part of Native American life in North America. But involvement with Europeans from the early seventeenth century on changed the nature of Indian war. In the centuries before the coming of whites, Indians rarely fought to annex territory or exclude rivals from trade routes. Indian wars were brief, and not very bloody. The commonest cause of war was revenge. In a village that had suffered a loss at the hands of outsiders, members of the victim's clan would organize a war party to punish the offenders. Participation in that war party was strictly voluntary, but bereaved family members had the right to insist that their male kinfolk provide them with a substitute for the lost husband, son, or brother in the form of either a captive or a scalp. That demand could not be refused without loss of honor. The object of war was to seize captives or take scalps without losing any men, so stealth and skill in ambush were highly esteemed. After the war party brought captives back to the village, those unfortunates were often put to death through slow torture—generally by burning—and were expected to endure their suffering stoically and even defiantly. Warriors memorized "death songs" to be sung to the enemy should it be their fate to face such an ordeal. But captives were not always killed. Some were enslaved, and others were adopted into the tribe, for family members had the right to claim them as replacements for the men they had lost. Revenge and replacement were not, however, the sole factors driving Indian warfare. A man's prestige depended on his skill as a warrior, so the young sought occasions to raid or pick quarrels with potential enemies.

The comments of European observers on Indian warfare in the early years of colonization are contradictory. On the one hand, they deplored Indian ferocity and brutality, portraying Native Americans as murderous savages who did not value peace. On the other hand, both the French and the British complained that Indians were poor soldiers, prone to leave the field of battle after they had taken a few scalps and captives. In the early seventeenth century, an English militia commander in New England sneered that the Pequots, reputed to be so ferocious, "might fight seven years and not kill seven men." The colonizers did not understand that the purpose of Indian warfare was not to kill as many of the enemy as possible, but to restore balance and harmony by exacting vengeance and securing restitution for real or imagined wrongs. At the same time, participation in war parties offered males opportunities to prove or confirm their manhood. The aggressive violence which in Europe might be expressed by the sacking of a city in the Native American world was focused on a few captives of war. Destruction of villages and killing of women, children, and the aged, while not totally unknown, were very uncommon in traditional Indian warfare. Roger Williams, the founder of Rhode Island, wrote that Indian wars "are far less bloody, and devouring, than the cruel wars of Europe."[12]

A New Kind of War

Although there is some disagreement among scholars about the reasons, the records of the early contact period leave no doubt that Native American warfare became more violent and destructive after the coming of whites. Raiding parties now sometimes destroyed entire villages, killing inhabitants indiscriminately. In some cases, entire populations were displaced. To cite a particularly extreme example, Iroquois warriors in the mid-seventeenth century drove most of the indigenous peoples out of what is now northern Ohio, and also decimated the Georgian Bay region of Ontario (home of the Huron, to whom they were closely related). The refugees resettled in the upper Great Lakes region, near Green Bay, Wisconsin, and did not reoccupy their former homelands in Ohio until after Iroquois power waned in the early eighteenth century. Increases in the violence of intertribal war are found in less extreme form throughout the continent.

One factor explaining new patterns in Indian warfare was the need to control trade. As local furbearing animals were hunted to extinction, tribes fought their neighbors and even rather distant peoples to gain access to pelts. The Iroquois and the Huron were trade rivals. By the early 1630s, both had exterminated local beaver populations, and sought to control trade with peoples to the north and west who were able to supply furs. The Iroquois, armed with guns by their Dutch trading partners, attacked the Hurons in 1649 and drove them from their homelands in the Georgian Bay region.

Fur pelts and deerskins were the primary, but not the only, items of trade that triggered conflict. In the southeast a flourishing commerce in

Indian slaves arose in the late seventeenth century, with Indian slave catchers selling other Indians to English merchants, who in turn shipped them for resale in New England or the Caribbean. The Indian slave trade was behind several very nasty Indian wars in the south. Loss of life through disease or warfare was also a cause of renewed Indian wars, as the bereaved sought captives to replace the dead. It is also possible that the despair produced by the great epidemics, and the loss in those catastrophes of much that held society together, explain the changes in warfare. But some of the warfare requires no new explanations. Native American males still needed to demonstrate courage and confirm manhood through heroic exploits.

Native Americans and European colonizers both actively sought to use each other as a military ally. To understand Indian and Euro-American behavior in the French and Indian War, it must be remembered that from the first years of contact, Indians and Europeans were intimately involved in one another's wars. In 1609, Samuel de Champlain assisted the Indians from the St. Lawrence valley in an attack on Iroquois at the lake which bears his name and, through use of French firepower, helped them gain an easy victory. In the same year, Powhatan at Jamestown sought to find a way to use the English and their fearful war machines to support his bid for power in the region. No European colony in North America—French, Dutch, English, or Spanish—could have survived without Indian military support. And no Indian village could be without guns or without European friends. In the European competition for empire, Indians did much of the fighting from the very first. It does not follow, however, that they were mere pawns of the colonists. Their leaders always sought ways to preserve their own independence, and often played one colonial power against another. Bear that in mind as you consider, in the chapters that follow, English and French relationships with their Indian allies.

A New Political Order

When the French and English colonies were founded in the seventeenth century, Native American peoples in eastern North America generally lived in decentralized, village-based communities held together by kinship and clan membership. For reasons not clearly understood, the hierarchical and urbanized Mississippian temple mound cultures of the great interior river valleys had disappeared by 1700. Although the League of the Iroquois and a few other confederations had developed some institutional structures that cut across village boundaries, Indians possessed no real equivalent of the European monarchy or nation-state. Their leaders were weak, and seldom wielded any authority outside their immediate area. Indian disunity and lack of much sense of ethnic identity placed them at a disadvantage in dealing with the more disciplined, tightly organized newcomers. But Native American political life was not static. In response to the new dangers and new opportunities that accompanied their growing involvement with European traders, merchants, missionaries, and soldiers, new leaders emerged who unified previously disunited peoples. Some, like the early eighteenth-century Creek leader Brims, were skilled diplomats who manipulated and maneuvered their European partners. Some, like Brims's successor Alexander McGillvray, were the children of European traders and Indian mothers, who knew how to operate in both worlds and used those skills for both personal benefit and the good of their people. Others, like the Ottawa chief Pontiac, who led an uprising shortly after the end of the French and Indian War, were nativists who fought to rid their homeland of white intruders. All, however, responded in one way or another to the European presence. Through their efforts, previously disunited peoples gradually formed Indian tribes and nations.

Native American Peoples in the French and Indian War

The Indian chiefs, warriors, and clan matrons who pondered the question of what to do as war broke out anew between Great Britain and France in North America were not savages, noble or otherwise, untouched by civilization. They and their parents and ancestors had been intimately involved with colonists for over a century and a half. They had been profoundly affected by that involvement. Most were well aware that one choice not available to them was to ignore Europeans and live a life untainted by their presence. Even in villages on the distant frontiers of the upper Great Lakes or the Illinois country, far from any British or French settlement, the white trader was a familiar figure. The closer they were to centers of European settlement, the greater the dependence of Indians on whites. But it was not a one-sided dependence, because as colonists faced a resumption of the ongoing great Anglo-French war for empire, for both sides the need for the goodwill (and, particularly in the case of the French, for the military aid) of Indians once again became acute. Each of the Native American peoples had its own distinctive history of interactions with colonizers, and each based its current decisions at least in part on old or recent memories. Contrary to the all too common stereotype, Native American leaders and their supporters were not simpleminded, primitive folk who were easily manipulated. As we will see in the chapters that follow, the decisions they made in their dealings with the European belligerents may have been wrongheaded on occasion, but they were most often driven by that most common of human motives: calculated self-interest.

Notes

1. For several very different assessments of Indian population, see Henry F. Dobyns, *Their Number Become Thinned: Native American Population Dynamics in Eastern North America* (Knoxville: University of Tennessee Press, 1983); Russell Thornton, *American Indian Holocaust and Survival: A Population History Since 1492* (Norman: University of Oklahoma Press, 1987); and David Henige, *Numbers from Nowhere: The American Indian Contact Population Debate* (Norman: University of Oklahoma Press, 1998).

2. Quoted in Alfred A. Cave, "Richard Hakluyt's Savages: The Influence of 16th Century Travel Narratives on English Policy in North America," *International Social Science Review,* 60 (Winter 1985): 16.

3. Thomas Morton, *The New English Canaan* (London, 1637), 18–19.

4. Colin G. Calloway, ed., *The World Turned Upside Down: Indian Voices from Early America* (Boston: St. Martin's Press, 1994), 4.

5. Thomas Gage to Lord Hillsborough, October 10, 1770, in *The Correspondence of Thomas Gage with the Secretaries of State,* 2 vols. (New Haven, CT: Yale University Press, 1931), 1:278.

6. Denys Delâge, *Bitter Feast: Amerindians and Europeans in Northeastern North America, 1600–64* (Vancouver: University of British Columbia Press, 1993), 63.

7. Shepard Krech III, *The Ecological Indian: Myth and History* (New York: Norton, 1999).

8. Delâge, *Bitter Feast,* 67–68.

9. Quotations from Colin G. Calloway, *New Worlds for All: Indians, Europeans and the Remaking of Early America* (Baltimore: Johns Hopkins University Press, 1997), 16–17.

10. Reuben Gold Thwaites, ed., *The Jesuit Relations and Allied Documents*, 78 vols. (Cleveland: Burrow Brothers, 1896–1901), 61:201–32.

11. Quoted in Kathryn E. Holland Braund, *Deerskins & Duffels: Creek Indian Trade with Anglo-America, 1685–1815* (Lincoln: University of Nebraska Press, 1993), 30.

12. Quoted in Alfred A. Cave, *The Pequot War* (Amherst: University of Massachusetts Press, 1996), 39, 153.

CHAPTER 3

THE FRENCH AND THE INDIANS: UNEASY PARTNERS

On the eve of the French and Indian War, some of Louis XV's advisers believed that France might need to abandon Canada. The colony was an economic liability. Exports from New France were worth only about a quarter of the cost of the commodities it had to import from France each year. Half of those exports, in value, were beaver skins obtained through the Indian trade; the rest consisted of fish oil and some agricultural products. None of the Canadian commodities were essential to the French economy. Tax revenues covered only about a tenth of the cost of governing and defending the colony. The problem was exacerbated by the corruption that was rampant in the colonial government. Shortly after arriving in Canada in 1756, General Louis Montcalm declared: "What a country, where all the knaves grow rich and honest men are ruined!"[1] Two years earlier, Intendant Francois Bigot, the official in charge of New France's finances, had received a letter from Paris warning that if the colony were not run more economically, the king would order that it be evacuated.[2]

New France's Vulnerability

Although the skeptics did not at first prevail, their reservations about the wisdom of continuing to invest in New France are understandable, if shortsighted. French Canada was sparsely populated. There were only two cities of any size—Quebec and Montreal—and those were small in comparison with Boston and New York. The colony lacked a critical mass of permanent French settlers. While Britain's North American colonies in 1754 boasted a population well in excess of a million, Canada's colonists numbered only 55,000. Twice as many French settlers lived in the Caribbean sugar islands—which, unlike Canada, were very profitable.

Some writers have suggested that had the Huguenots (French Protestants) been allowed to settle in New France, the outcome of the French and Indian War might have been different. In their view, the French monarchy's decision to restrict access to the colony to Roman Catholics stifled its growth. While the Huguenots, who made important contributions to the British colonies where they did settle, would no doubt have been an asset to New France, we nonetheless need to be skeptical of the claim that their exclusion explains France's defeat in North America. Huguenot immigrants would not have been numerous enough to cancel out Britain's overwhelming advantage in population. Moreover, Canada's vulnerability was more than a matter of numbers. The colony's economic base was weak. On the eve of the French and Indian War, crop failures and food shortages plagued Canada's colonial administrators, who at times found it difficult to provision the garrisons of the frontier forts. The governor, Ange Duquesne de Menneville, on one occasion, had to supply his army by seizing grain at bayonet point from hungry habitants (settlers) suffering from a bad harvest. Ironically, shortly before mounting their campaign against the English in the Ohio country, the French in Canada found it necessary to buy food from the British merchants of New York and New England. Harvests failed twice during the crucial war years—in 1757 and in 1758—while the British naval blockade made it nearly impossible to bring in badly needed foodstuffs from France. The defenders of Canada were often hungry. Corrupt local officials, led by Bigot, exacerbated the grain shortage by speculation, hoarding, and price gouging.[3]

The Decision to Defend Canada

Despite those difficulties, the French government, committed to the defense of far-flung colonial possessions, including lucrative sugar-producing islands of the Caribbean, decided that Canada could play an important role in checking British ambitions in the Americas and must therefore be held despite the cost. In 1750 the case for defending Canada had been spelled out in a memorandum to the authorities in Paris from a former governor of New France, the marquis de la Galissonière. The marquis declared that in principle, "honor, glory and religion forbid the abandonment of a colony." In more practical terms, he argued that control of

Canada was essential not only for the security of French holdings in Louisiana and the Caribbean but also for the protection of the New World possessions of France's ally Spain from British aggression.[4]

The advocates of an aggressive policy in North America realized that the French in Canada were greatly outnumbered by their British rivals to the south, but they saw in alliances with Indian nations the means of winning a war fought on the northern border and on the western frontier. The support of the Indian nations of North America in the past had neutralized the English advantage. There was no reason why Indian warriors could not once again be called to the defense of New France. The French government did not take seriously the possibility that Great Britain might take Canada by force. Past history encouraged complacency. In previous wars, no British colonial army had succeeded in penetrating the St. Lawrence valley. Navigation of the river was exceedingly difficult. The land route could easily be defended with the help of Indian auxiliaries. The expectation that France would receive crucial support from the Indians played a central role in French plans for a war against the British in North America.

The government in Paris, preoccupied with the power struggle in Europe, never intended to make a major investment in the defense of Canada. They hoped that the Indians, with the support of the Canadian militia, could carry most of the burden. Galissonière had assured French officials that the Indians were firmly tied to France by self-interest, for they understood that it was important in maintaining their independence that "the strength of the English and the French remain essentially equal." They had served as excellent tutors to the French traders, who, unlike the English, "were accustomed to live in the woods like Indians" and could wage war in the Indian manner. French Canadians and Indians together, he argued, could easily defeat the British.[5]

As we have seen, the former governor's analysis was flawed. Indians proved to be less reliable than expected, and the British far more adept as frontier warriors. But the early years of the conflict appeared to confirm Galissonière's prediction. In 1756, from Fort Carillon (Ticonderoga) in New York, a young French captain wrote to his father in France: "The English colonies have ten times more people than ours; but these wretches have not the least knowledge of war, and if they go out to fight, they must abandon wives, children, and all they possess." France's Indian allies, the captain related, were decimating the enemy. "It is incredible what a quantity of scalps they bring us. In Virginia they have committed unheard of cruelties, carried off families, burned a great many houses and killed an infinity of people. These miserable English are in the extremity of distress, and repent too late the unjust war they began against us. It is a pleasure to make war in Canada."[6]

New France's Catholic Indians

The captain's observations underscore the importance of Indian allies to the French war effort. The relationship of French Canadians to Canada's "First Nations" has often been romanticized and frequently misrepresented. In one of those sweeping and often quoted generalizations that both illuminate and distort, the great nineteenth-century historian Francis Parkman declared, "Spanish civilization crushed the Indian; English civilization scorned and neglected him; French civilization embraced and cherished him."[7] In all three cases the relationships of Indians to colonizers were actually far more complex. But in eastern Canada, Catholic missionaries, particularly the Jesuits, did achieve some successes by "embracing" Native Americans, and came to "cherish" them as irreplaceable allies. While Protestant missionaries in the English colonies insisted that to accept Christ, Indians must give up their traditional beliefs, customs, and practices and live like Europeans, the French "Black Robes" brought their Indian charges into the Catholic fold without demanding that they abandon their cultural identity.

In the eastern St. Lawrence valley the missionaries established a number of "praying villages" inhabited by Indian converts who embraced the Catholic faith but retained many aspects of their traditional way of life. In those settlements, unlike comparable "praying villages" in Puritan New England, Indians were not forced to conform totally to European standards of dress, deportment, and behavior. Rather than relying on interpreters, the missionaries learned the Indian languages. To reach those Indians who did not live near the French settlements on the St. Lawrence River, the French dispatched missionaries to live in Indian villages. Father Sebastian Rasles, one of the most influential eighteenth-century French missionaries, spent thirty years in an Abenaki village at Norridgewock, Maine. In explaining his success, Rasles wrote that he conformed to "their manners and customs, to the end that I might gain their confidence and win them to Jesus Christ."[8] Some years earlier, Father Jerome Lalement had declared that to succeed, the missionary must first have "penetrated their thoughts . . . adapted himself to their manner of living and, when necessary, been a Barbarian with them."[9]

The techniques employed by New France's missionaries in winning converts were both distinctive and controversial. While members of the more conservative Recollet order disapproved of compromises with paganism, the Jesuits achieved great success by finding parallels between Catholic and Native American spiritual practices. They relied on rituals that could easily resonate with the sense of awe, mystery, and magic that was characteristic of Native American spirituality. They made extensive use of visual and auditory symbols in worship, communicating by means of pictures, incense, bells, and candelight something of the mystical richness as well as the teachings of Catholicism. Unlike their far less successful Puritan counterparts in New England, they required only minimal understanding of theology. To draw Indians into the Catholic fold, they found ways to adapt Christian practices to Native American usage. Thus Native Americans, who generally believed in the magical powers of amulets or other extraordinary objects, were given religious medals and rings. They were told also of the blessings that came to those who knelt before crucifixes, prayed the rosary, or venerated relics. Under the tutelage of the fathers, neophyte Indian Christians destroyed their traditional medicine bundles and replaced them with Christian objects that they expected would also be sources of good luck and of power.

In common with other colonial era missionaries, Catholic and Protestant alike, most Jesuits hoped in time to eliminate all vestiges of Indian superstition. In actual practice, however, the religious observances and folk beliefs of New France's Catholic Indians blended the old and the new. One historian has concluded: "Indians were not so much being converted to Christianity as Christ was being converted into a manitou [Indian spirit being]."[10] Some of the Jesuits were not particularly bothered by that, for they saw in Native American beliefs glimmerings of divine truth. Father Lalemont, reporting on missionary work in 1647, declared: "It is certain that all men are created to know, to love, and to enjoy their God, but very diversely."[11] Others were less optimistic. They were disturbed by the lack of discipline and the lack of deference to authority that persisted in Native American life even after exposure to Catholic teaching, and suspected the continued presence of the diabolical. One priest complained that the Indian languages lacked "all words for piety, devotion, virtue," as well as "all terms which are used to express the things of the other life."[12] Even Lalemont deplored widespread Indian resistance to the discipline of the Catholic Church, and regretted that force could not be used "to curb the insolence of those who trample under foot the holiness of her Mysteries."[13]

Gathering converts in villages under the direction of a priest, or sending a priest to live in their communities, the missionaries incorporated members of the eastern Canadian Indian nations—Montagnais, Abenaki, Algonquin, and others—into the institutional fabric of New France. Although culturally not French, they shared with the newcomers some aspects of a common faith. The converts who lived in the "praying villages" are sometimes referred to as the "domiciled Indians." They were New France's most reliable military allies. While the fathers disapproved of many aspects of Native American warfare (for example, the wars of personal revenge, the practice of torturing and sometimes cannibalizing captives), they were not pacifists. They hoped to transform their Indian converts into proper Christian warriors ready to do battle against the British heretics.

French efforts to convert and to recruit Indian allies were not limited to Canada, but also included sending missionaries south into territories claimed by Great Britain. The Jesuits in particular worked assiduously to win converts among the Iroquois. It is estimated that two-thirds of the Mohawks left New York in the late seventeenth and early eighteenth centuries to settle at Caugnawagas, a Catholic missionary village near Montreal. The Jesuits later made inroads among the Cayugas and Onondagas as well, many of whom gathered at a mission established in 1749 at Swegatchy, on the site of the modern town of Ogdensburg, New York. The Senecas, whose homeland in western New York was closest to Canada, had long had Jesuit priests in residence. Shortly before the outbreak of the French and Indian War, the Senecas welcomed Louis Thomas de Joncaire, a French officer charged with winning over the western Indians. The presence in each of the Iroquois nations of a pro-French faction reinforced the League's neutrality policy and helped thwart British efforts to recruit the Iroquois as allies in the invasion of Canada.

New France's Indian Warriors

In each of the colonial wars, the domiciled Indians joined French Canadian soldiers in raiding English settlements on the northern frontier, burning farms and towns, killing many of their inhabitants, and carrying others into captivity. New England in particular was hard hit. From the late seventeenth century on, frontier warfare adversely affected the region's territorial expansion, population growth, and economic development. New York City flourished at Boston's expense. Although not immune, the New York colony was often spared the worst of the fighting. In fact, throughout the eighteenth century New Yorkers commonly continued to trade with Montreal, through Albany, even when Great Britain and France were at war. But New England always faced the full fury of the enemy.

The profound sense of dread inspired by Indian raiders in New England is illustrated in a strange episode at Gloucester, Massachusetts, during King William's War. In broad daylight in mid-July 1692, the town's sentries fired their muskets at what they believed was a small band of blue-coated Frenchmen guiding a great horde of Indians with "black bushy hair" toward the village. In panic, the sentries cried for reinforcements. But when they came, no French soldiers and no Indians could be found. It had been an illusion—but one that tells us much about the psychology of the French and Indian wars.[14] In 1745, the governor of New France reported that the British were afraid to occupy some of the land they claimed in Acadia (Nova Scotia) because of their "dread of the Indians."[15] In fact, the vast hordes of savages imagined by frightened British colonists did not exist. New France's eastern Indians, decimated by disease in the previous century, were few in number, and by some estimates could field no more than a thousand warriors. Their impact upon the balance of power on the frontier had been quite remarkable in years past. But they would not play a comparable role in the final "French and Indian War."

The French and the Western Indian Nations

The mission Indians of the lower St. Lawrence valley and the relocated Iroquois converts who joined them in Canada were not typical. Most of the Indians of New France never really embraced Catholicism, although for practical reasons they usually tolerated missionaries or pretended to convert. The native peoples of northern and western Canada at first were not much impressed by the French holy men. The Black Robes struck them at best as strange, ineffectual men without useful skills. They were not hunters or warriors. They wore strange garb not suitable for life and work in the woods and on the waters. Their commitment to celibacy seemed peculiar, and rather sinister. Soon Indians came to suspect that the missionary priests were witches responsible for bringing disease and death to their villages. The Huron, one scholar relates, generally believed "that the Jesuits were the agents by which epidemics were being spread. No other reason could account more plausibly for why the French had insisted that these priests be allowed to live in the Huron country. Their celibacy also suggested that they were nurturing great supernatural power, and their generally sound health and the speed with which they and their workmen recovered from influenza were additional proofs that they could control these diseases."[16]

Fear of Jesuit "witchcraft" sometimes led to martyrdom as frightened Indians sought to protect themselves by killing those whom they believed responsible for the unexplained increase in mortality. But the French generally insisted that their trading partners welcome missionaries and allow them to live in their villages. Tribal councils on several occasions backed away from ordering the killing of priests as witches when they pondered the consequences of loss of French trade. Moreover, the French sold goods to Catholic converts at lower cost than they charged Indians who remained "pagan." They also refused to provide non-Christians with access to guns. Western Indians, in order to acquire firearms and other necessities, not only tolerated priests in their midst but also sometimes falsely claimed to be converts. Even so, French missionary endeavors outside the eastern St. Lawrence watershed were not particularly successful.

The link that joined most of Canada's Indian nations to the French was not a common faith but a common interest in the fur trade. On the eve of the French and Indian War, the French government maintained some forty-four fortified Indian trading posts, some protected by a small garrison. Of those, twenty-eight were located in the upper Great Lakes region.[17] These posts gave France a substantial strategic advantage in the early years of the war. Although British traders had been active in the west for over a decade, the British had not built permanent fortifications in the contested territories.

New France had originally been founded to protect France's interest in the offshore fisheries of the Newfoundland banks. In the seventeenth century French policy makers had not encouraged French settlers to engage directly in the fur trade, preferring to deal instead with Indian middlemen. In 1680, Louis XIV had issued an order restricting travel in Indian country, fearing that in the wilderness colonists would be corrupted by "savages," and would thereafter neglect the "agriculture, commerce, manufactures and other profitable enterprises" which were needed to place the colony on a firm economic footing.[18] But French officials in Canada soon recognized that the fur trade not only was their main source of profit but also was essential to winning and holding the loyalties of the Indian nations. Soon French traders penetrated the most remote regions of Canada, and came to replace Indian middlemen in the quest to tap the still unexhausted fur reserves of the backcountry. True to the fears of monarchy and church, the traders often embraced an Indian lifestyle and very commonly took Indian wives. They were probably more effective than the priests in tying the interests of the western Indians to France.

The French were not acknowledged as overlords or rulers west of the St. Lawrence valley; the "far Indians" of the upper Great Lakes and Old Northwest prized their independence. But French traders and diplomats did come to play a very special role not only as suppliers of essential trade goods but also as mediators among rivals and adversaries. They were incorporated as" fathers" or "uncles" into Native American diplomatic rituals grounded in fictive kinship. They enjoyed great prestige, and much was also expected of them. The west was, as one historian terms it, a "middle ground," a meeting place of cultures where the usual assumptions about colonial rule and aboriginal subordination simply did not apply.[19] The Indians of the Great Lakes and other western regions valued the French for three reasons: (1) their posts and forts offered an easily accessible source of trade goods; (2) French officials were useful as mediators of inter-tribal disputes; (3) since the French were few in number, they were far less of a threat to Indian security and landownership than were the British. Indians were acutely aware of British land greed. Many had bitter memories of the loss of their homelands as British settlers forced them into exile in the west. The French sought their trade, and their support in war, but were not sufficiently numerous to threaten their hold on their land. That made them more attractive as allies than their British rivals. That does not necessarily mean that the French were always trusted. The Indians of the Ohio valley frequently expressed suspicion that both the English and the French planned to steal their land. But, as one Delaware leader put it, the British were "such a numerous people" that it made sense to use the

French against them. Should any problems arise at a later time, the chief declared, "we can drive the French away when we please."[20]

Unmanageable Allies

In assessing the Indian contribution to the French war effort, bear in mind that most Indian warriors, even many from "praying villages," did not consider themselves soldiers in the service of the king of France. They prized their freedom. They honored their own customs of warfare. Those customs, which placed particular value on individual courage and also emphasized the taking of captives, scalps, and booty, often came into conflict with French military needs and plans. Let us examine a few examples.

Although Baron Ludwig Dieskau, commander of the French army that invaded New York in 1755, possessed a rare understanding of the value of irregular forces, his experiences in trying to lead Indians into battle exposed the fallacy of the belief that Native American support would compensate for France's manpower deficiency in North America. Indian warriors were generally not willing to engage in protracted siege warfare. They were accustomed to short campaigns and direct action. They were also fiercely independent and not accustomed to regimentation. They proved to be unmanageable allies. During Dieskau's campaign against William Johnson in 1755, none of the Indians who accompanied his army were willing to join in the siege of Fort Edward. For that reason, Dieskau had to change his battle plans. Then, after Johnson's forces fell into the ambush the baron had set for them on the road leading to the fort, the Caugnawaga Mohawks refused to obey his order to attack Johnson's camp. Their reason: many of their New York Mohawk relatives were with the English there, and they did not want to kill kinfolk. The Abenakis then refused to proceed without Mohawks. Deprived of Indian auxiliaries, the Canadian militia also declined to fight. Only the French regulars were willing to obey Dieskau's order to attack. The attack failed. The baron was wounded and taken prisoner.

His successor had even more problems with Indian auxiliaries. Some of his contemporaries and a number of later historians have faulted Montcalm for his lack of understanding of Native Americans. Montcalm's campaign against Fort William Henry in 1757 exposed not only his personal deficiencies but also both the cultural gap dividing the allies and the essential fragility of Indian support for New France. Montcalm had little respect for Indians. Shortly after his arrival in Canada, the general wrote to his mother: "You would not believe it, but the men always carry to war, along with their tomahawk and gun, a mirror to dab their faces with various colors, and arrange feathers on their heads and rings in their noses. They think it a great beauty to cut the rim of the ear and stretch it till it reaches the shoulder. Often they wear a laced coat, with no shirt at all. You would take them for so many masqueraders or devils. One needs the patience of an angel to get on with them."[21]

After the victory at Fort William Henry, Montcalm's Indian allies, gathered from over thirty nations, felt cheated when the general paroled the British garrison, and were deeply angered when he tried to intervene to keep them from taking captives. Having fought well and risked their lives for the French, the Indians believed that they had won the right to captives, loot, and scalps. To return to their villages without such evidence of their success in battle would be disgraceful. They did not understand French behavior. One warrior declared to a French officer: "I made war for plunder, scalps and prisoners. You are satisfied with a fort, and you let your enemy and mine live. I do not want to keep such bad meat for tomorrow. When I kill it, it can no longer attack me."[22] The French, Indians complained, were now conspiring with the British to deprive them of the fruits of victory.

The French, too, were unhappy. Their Indian allies, some French officers complained, were inhumane, prone to abuse prisoners, given to torture, scalping, and even, on occasion, ritual cannibalism. Even worse, they were unreliable, and would often return to their home villages after taking a few prisoners. The French Canadians, for their part, were often short of food, and therefore resented the cost of feeding the warriors who responded to the call to fight against the British. The relationship of soldiers and settlers to Indian warriors was seldom easy and often strained. Tensions also developed among French army troops, the local colonial standing army, and the French Canadian militia. Montcalm distrusted the local forces, and clashed with his nominal superior, the Canadian-born Governor Pierre Vaudreuil, on overall strategy. In 1759, Paris ordered the governor to defer to the general on military matters. But Montcalm's failure to hold together the army, the militia, and the Indian allies crippled the French offensive in New York and helped pave the way to defeat.

Of the 1,200 Indian warriors who responded to the call to join Montcalm's offensive against New York in 1758, about a fourth were from the west. They had been attracted by promises that there would be great spoils to be had by fighting the British. However, they not only returned to their home villages bitterly resentful that Montcalm had deprived them of the material rewards of victory, but also brought with them smallpox. Soon an epidemic decimated the western villages. Very few western Indians fought for the French thereafter. The spread of smallpox convinced many of them that they were victims of French malice and witchcraft. The Menominees in Wisconsin even attacked a French fort in their territory.

The domiciled Indians—Abenaki, Nipissing, Algonquin—from the mission villages of Quebec also were disaffected, sharing with the westerners the belief that Montcalm had cheated them. Soon after taking Fort William Henry, the general found himself without Indian auxiliaries, and no longer felt able to continue his campaign. After burning the fort, Montcalm returned to Canada. A year later, as he sought to defend Fort Carillon (Ticonderoga) against a British offensive, only 16 out of an estimated 800 warriors in eastern Canada responded to his call. Although many were nominally Catholic, those warriors remained Indians in their concept of the rules of war.

The absence of Indian scouts to fan through the woods, attack British rangers, gather intelligence, and wage guerrilla war against English outposts crippled the French army in New York. Montcalm and the other French commanders were now constrained to apply a conventional European strategy to defend their holdings. New France had lost her military advantage, and soon faced a series of defeats.

It would be an oversimplification, however, to attribute the Indian decision to withdraw to anger over Montcalm's attitude or to his behavior at Fort William Henry. The Indian nations of the west and of the Ohio valley, whose support was vital to the realization of France's objectives in North America, were never bound to France by ties of religion or personal loyalty. They were motivated by self-interest. There were two things they needed from a European ally: trade on reasonable terms and protection from those who wanted to take their land away from them. Early in the war, it appeared that the French would offer both, but the tightening of the British naval blockade led to severe shortages of French trade goods by 1758. Also decisive in persuading the western Indians to make peace with the British were recurrent reports of British success on the battlefield. The backwoods intelligence networks operated with remarkable speed and efficiency. By 1759, it was apparent that the French were losing the war. A loser could not provide trade goods, let alone protection. Soon most of the Indians in the crucial frontier arc from New York though the Ohio country withdrew from the war. The "far Indians" of the west, with whom Montcalm had clashed in 1757, remained disillusioned. Indian desertion of the French cause doomed hopes for French control of the Ohio country, and placed New France itself in danger. Catholic mission Indians in eastern Canada for a time assisted in the defense of Quebec in 1759, but after the fall of the city, even they made peace with the invaders and played no role in the final battles in 1760.

France Abandons Canada

With New France's erstwhile Indian allies now opting for neutrality, and with the Iroquois once again British allies, the last stages of the defense of Canada would be mounted primarily by regular army troops and colonial militia. Despite the British advantage in numbers, the invasion and pacification of Canada was a daunting task. British attempts to take Canada in previous wars had failed. Could New France have been saved? Perhaps, if France had committed substantial numbers of fresh troops from Europe to her defense. But, quite apart from the question of whether the French government valued Canada sufficiently to divert resources needed elsewhere, British naval superiority at this point proved decisive. In 1759, France lost the battle of Quiberon Bay in Brittany. With much of her navy sunk, France could not effectively challenge the British blockade and re-supply Canada. The local population was too small, and its resources too limited, to mount a new offensive and drive the occupiers from Quebec and Niagara. Finally, Montreal also fell, and the French governor acknowledged defeat in 1760.

But the world war was not over. Although France fared poorly in the battles of the next two years, the cost of war drove a new British government to seek a negotiated peace. France did not surrender unconditionally. Peace was restored only after some horse-trading at the conference table. In previous Anglo-French wars, American territory lost in battle had been restored to France by treaty. Some thought perhaps Canada would be given back in exchange for other concessions. It did not happen. Instead, the French regained their Caribbean sugar islands but gave up New France. Many Frenchmen, looking at the commercial balance sheets, believed they had saved the more valuable part of the empire in that transaction. Étienne Francois, duke of Choiseul, the French negotiator of the Peace of Paris in 1763, later boasted about his cleverness in persuading the British to return the Antilles in exchange for the permanent cession of Canada. The great philosopher Voltaire quipped that Louis XV had lost nothing more than "a few acres of snow."[23] They were right only in the short run. That assessment of the outcome of the French and Indian War reflected not wisdom but ignorance of the true potential of North America.

Notes

1. Quoted in Noel St. John Williams, *Redcoats Along the Hudson* (London: Brassy's, 1998), 124.

2. Lawrence Henry Gipson, *The British Empire Before the American Revolution,* 12 vols. (New York: Alfred A. Knopf, 1958–70), 5:24–27.

3. Ibid., 5:33; Fred Anderson, *Crucible of War* (New York: Alfred A. Knopf, 2000), 236.

4. E.B. O'Callaghan and B. Fernow, eds., *Documents Relative to the Colonial History of the State of New York,* 15 vols. (Albany, NY: Weed and Parsons, 1853–87), 10:320–32.

5. Ibid.

6. Quoted in Francis B. Parkman, *Montcalm and Wolfe* (New York: Da Capo Press, 1995), 220–21.

7. Francis Parkman, "Jesuits of New France," in *France and England in North America*, 2 vols. (New York: Library of America, 1983), 2:432.

8. Quoted in Colin G. Calloway, *New Worlds for All* (Baltimore: Johns Hopkins University Press, 1997), 89.

9. Reuben Gold Thwaites, ed., *The Jesuit Relations and Allied Documents,* 78 vols. (Cleveland: Burrow Brothers, 1896–1901), 23:207–9.

10. Richard White, *The Middle Ground* (New York: Cambridge University Press, 1991), 45.

11. Thwaites, *Jesuit Relations,* 31:231.

12. Ibid., 7:21.

13. Ibid., 18:55.

14. Samuel Niles, "A Summary Historical Narrative of the Wars in New-England with the French and the Indians," *Massachusetts Historical Society Collections,* 3rd ser., 6 (1836):231–32.

15. O'Callaghan and Fernow, *Documents,* 10:14.

16. Bruce G. Trigger, *Natives and Newcomers: Canada's "Heroic Age" Reconsidered* (Montreal: McGill-Queen's University Press, 1985), 246.

17. Gipson, *British Empire Before the American Revolution,* 5:52.

18. Ibid., 5:44.

19. White, *The Middle Ground.*

20. Ibid., 244–45.

21. Quoted in Parkman, *Montcalm and Wolfe,* 216–17.

22. Quoted in Ian K. Steele, *Betrayals: Fort William Henry and the "Massacre"* (New York: Oxford University Press, 1990), 131.

23. Quoted in Frank W. Brecher, *Losing a Continent* (Westport, CT: Greenwood Press, 1998), 19.

CHAPTER 4

BRITISH COLONISTS AND NATIVE AMERICANS: TROUBLED RELATIONSHIPS

In 1755 Edmund Atkin, superintendent of Indian affairs for the southern colonies, warned that the well-being of England's New World empire depended upon good relations with the Indians. "While they are our friends, they are the cheapest and strongest barrier for protection of our settlements." But, Atkin added, "when enemies," they were capable "of rendering those possessions almost useless."[1] The more perceptive British colonial officials shared Atkin's understanding that the empire could not afford to alienate the native inhabitants of North America. A few of the ill-informed—Edward Braddock and Jeffrey Amherst, for example—sometimes imagined that all Indians could easily be subjugated by a show of force. But from the earliest days of colonization, British officials in the colonies generally tried to conduct their relations with the Indian nations in such a way as to assure their help and support as trading partners and military allies. Through gift giving and subsidizing trade they sought to bind Indians to the colonists.

Making Indian Enemies: Crooked Traders, Land Grabbers, and Frontier Killers

Those ties were hard to maintain. In their day-to-day dealings with Native Americans, colonial governors, generals, and Indian agents often found it very difficult to match their good words with action. There were perennial problems with traders who cheated and abused their Indian customers. Although the majority of traders were probably honest and upright men, the documentary records of the colonial era are filled with complaints against traders who defrauded their customers with false weights and measures or plied them with liquor in order to steal their goods. Some sexually abused Indian women. Others sometimes beat or killed Indians they deemed uncooperative. The bad behavior of unscrupulous merchants in Indian country sometimes resulted in their deaths at the hands of their outraged victims and occasionally led to Indian wars. (To cite only one example, the Yamasee War of 1715 in the Carolinas was triggered by traders who seized and sold into slavery Indians who allegedly owed them money.) Colonial authorities lacked the means to police the frontier.[2] Regulation of the Indian trade was one of the unresolved problems in Great Britain's North American empire.

British colonial governments had even less control over the activities of backcountry settlers interested not in coexisting with Indians but in driving them from the land. The interests of Indians also often clashed with the aspirations of land companies, whose agents and investors used all manner of persuasion to induce tribesmen to relinquish land to make room for new English settlements. In some cases white land claimants and squatters drove Indians from their homes by force.

More than any other area of conflict, controversies over land undermined British professions of friendship for Indians. Between 1700 and 1760, the nonindigenous population of Britain's North American colonies increased fourfold, from 400,000 to 1,600,000. Great Britain was a crowded island of limited resources where the privileged few lived in comfort, most enjoyed only limited opportunities and faced some privations, while many others lived in abject poverty. Hence, each year thousands upon thousands of English emigrated to America in search of a better life. They were joined by immigrants from Ireland, Scotland, and the mainland of Europe, all drawn by the promise of the New World. These newcomers did not intend to live as they had in the Old World. They dreamed of becoming landowners, but by the mid-eighteenth century land on the Atlantic seaboard was no longer easily available to everyone. Driven by both need and ambition, the immigrants had little patience with restrictions against settling on Indian land, and little if any respect for Indian rights or, in some cases, even for Indian life. Native Americans, by their lights, had no real right to the land because they were said to be a savage, vicious, and backward people, few in number, lazy and shiftless in their habits. Thus, a group of aspiring Scots-Irish settlers petitioned the provincial secretary of Pennsylvania, stating that "it was against the laws of God and nature that so much land should be idle while so many Christians wanted it to labor on, and raise their bread."[3]

Within limits, Indian tribes generally were willing to try to accommodate the settlers. From the first years of contact they had granted or sold land to colonists, and often found land sales an easy way of erasing debts to traders or acquiring new trade goods. But by the eighteenth century some Indian leaders feared that whites intended to take all the land and leave them homeless. These leaders were determined to maintain the integrity of their remaining territories. But British frontiersmen more often than not refused to recognize their rights. The petition quoted above expresses a commonplace resentment of Indian retention of hunting preserves. Whites often argued that Indians should not be allowed to keep land they did not cultivate. When Andrew Jackson, born in 1767, told President James Monroe in 1817 that he considered it an "absurdity" to negotiate with "savages" over taking land that civilized people needed, he was expressing a frontier belief which was probably as old as the colonies.[4]

Colonial officials and British military authorities often complained about their inability to protect Native Americans from Indian-hating settlers. Sir William Johnson, Great Britain's superintendent of Indian affairs for the northern colonies, wrote of white intruders on Indian land: "Those who daily go over the Mountains of Virginia . . . have a hatred for, ill treat, Rob, and frequently murder the Indians."[5] When several Virginians imprisoned for killing Indians without provocation were freed by a mob in 1767, British General Thomas Gage complained, "All the people of the Frontiers from Pennsylvania to Virginia inclusive, openly avow, that they will never find a Man guilty of Murther [murder] for killing an Indian."[6] Confirming Gage's judgment, a year later a Pennsylvania mob forced the release from jail of a rum dealer named Frederick Stump who had murdered several of his Iroquois customers in cold blood. Stump was never punished for his crime. Several years earlier, Governor John Penn of Pennsylvania had complained, "No jury in any of our frontier counties will ever condemn a man for killing an Indian. They do not consider it murder, but as a meritorious act."[7] The great Shawnee resistance leader Tecumseh, expressing the fundamental reason for his distrust of Anglo-Americans, many years later declared: "They do not think the red man sufficiently good to live."[8] Random unprovoked killing of Indians, along with Indian fear of loss of their land to British settlers, often made it difficult for the British to recruit and hold Indian allies.

Winning Indian Friends: Frontier Diplomats and Cheap Trade Goods

The problems created by such incidents notwithstanding, the British nonetheless had certain advantages in the competition for Native American support. A handful of exceptionally able traders and forest diplomats, including Johann Conrad Weiser, Christian Frederick Post, George Croghan, and William Johnson, very skillfully repaired some of the damage done by white Indian haters. Those colonial Indian agents usually had Indian wives, often wore Indian garb, generally participated in tribal rituals, and frequently had been admitted to tribal membership. They understood not only the Indians' languages but also their needs and fears. Those insights enabled them to cross the cultural divide and explain "the Old World to the New."[9]

Admittedly, their good work was sometimes undone by the bungling of inept British commanders unfamiliar with the particular requirements of forest diplomacy and war. The ill-fated General Edward Braddock alienated the Delaware by telling Chief Shingas that no Indian had any right to inherit land. After the war, Lord Jeffrey Amherst's heavy-handed treatment of Indians helped to provoke Pontiac's rebellion. But British agents nonetheless had one truly formidable advantage in the competition for Indian support. British trade goods, coveted by Indian clients, were superior in quality and lower in cost than those supplied by the French. The British were able to resupply their Indian friends. The French in Canada, handicapped by a British naval blockade that created drastic shortages of goods, frequently could not. Thus, by 1759, most Indians who had supported France early in the war decided that they could no longer afford to do so.

Great Britain's victory in the French and Indian War is not surprising. The French in Canada numbered only 55,000; the population of the British colonies exceeded a million. What is surprising is that the contest was so close and the end so long in coming. Since Native Americans, contrary to the stereotype of the irrational savage, were realists, and generally gravitated to the most powerful of the European competitors for their favor, their long reluctance to support the British requires close scrutiny. Part of the reason is found in British and colonial misconduct of the war effort, a problem that will be addressed in chapter 5. But the answer is found also in the nature of past British interactions with prospective Indian allies. To understand that problem more clearly, we must look closely at several specific cases.

Case Study 1: The League of the Iroquois, England's Erstwhile Ally

British security and success in the French and Indian wars depended upon good relations with the powerful League of the Iroquois, a confederation of Indian nations occupying the strategically vital northern and western regions of New York. At the close of King William's War, the governor of New York had warned London that if the Iroquois should ever decide to fight for France, "the English would be forced off the continent in two months."[10] British policy makers understood that in all confrontations with the French in Canada, the Iroquois at minimum must be kept neutral. They also believed that the help of Iroquois warriors would make victory a certainty. But the close alliance between the English and the Iroquois that served New York so well in the seventeenth century was not renewed after 1701. To understand the reasons, we must look at Iroquois experiences as a military ally of England.

The League of the Iroquois was the most remarkable Native American political organization in eastern North America. It had been founded several centuries before the arrival of the first European. Although no one knows the exact date of his revelation, the Iroquois relate that, in a time of destructive warfare among Iroquois villages, a supernatural being called Deganawidah had taught the warrior Hiawatha certain rituals that would end the violence and restore peace. Inspired by the teachings of Deganawidah and Hiawatha, five Iroquoian tribes, speaking similar dialects and sharing a common culture, joined to form the League of the Iroquois. Sometimes called the Five Nations, the original members were the Mohawks, the Oneidas, the Onondagas, the Cayugas, and the Senecas. The Tuscaroras, Iroquoian-speaking refugees from the south, were admitted in 1722. The League thereafter was sometimes referred to as the Six Nations. Hoping to extend the covenant they termed "the Great Tree of Peace," the Iroquois often sought to persuade the nonmember nations they defeated in war to subscribe to the principles of the League and accept Iroquois guidance.

In the seventeenth century, the Iroquois allied first with the Dutch and then the English. From New Netherlands, the Dutch colony in the Hudson River valley founded in 1624, the Iroquois obtained guns, ammunition, and other war materials that made them a formidable adversary in the Indian world. Their quest for furs with which to purchase European trade goods soon led to the virtual extermination of furbearing animals close to home. In the 1640s the Iroquois waged the "Beaver Wars," a devastating series of attacks on rival Indian nations allied with France. The purpose of those raids in part was to gain control of the fur trade, but traditional war objectives, such as the acquisition of captives to replace dead kinsmen and the confirmation of masculinity through feats of bravery, remained powerful motivations. When England replaced Holland as the colonial power in New York, the Iroquois sought close ties with the newcomers. In 1677, those ties were formalized in a military and commercial alliance, a Covenant Chain that bound them together as equals committed to honor mutual obligations. With the encouragement of their English ally, Iroquois war parties terrorized France's Indian trading partners in the Ohio country, the upper Mississippi valley, and the Great Lakes.

The cost was high. It is estimated that in the last twenty years of the seventeenth century, the League members lost more than half their warriors. The Iroquois homeland itself was no longer secure. Counterattacking French and Indian forces devastated Iroquois villages in New York. When their English allies failed to provide protection, factions within the Iroquois nations favoring either a pact with the French or neutrality successfully challenged the English alliance. Throughout the first six decades of the eighteenth century, skepticism about English reliability remained a powerful deterrent to resumption of the former military relationship with them.

In 1701, the League made peace and entered into a trade agreement with the French at Montreal. But the Iroquois had no intention of trading one European ally for another; most Iroquois now wished to fight for neither. For that reason, the League also renewed in a different form their Covenant Chain with England. Iroquois representatives placated the English by granting to the king their rather questionable claim to ownership of extensive hunting territories in the west by right of conquest. They reserved the right to continue to send occasional hunting parties into those domains.

The key to the 1701 Iroquois settlement with England and France was military neutrality. Thereafter, while small, individual Iroquois war parties might sometimes fight on the side of the English or the French, the Confederation (as the diplomatic and military arm of the League, established after the coming of Europeans, was sometimes called) remained officially aloof from Europe's colonial wars. Although New York negotiators came close to reestablishing a military alliance with the Iroquois during both Queen Anne's War and King George's War, the colonists' failure in both wars to match words with deeds and mount an effective invasion of Canada persuaded Iroquois statesmen that the British colonists were still unreliable. They did not want to risk offending the French unless a British victory was certain. Neutrality also spared the League's members from fighting against kinsmen who were pro-French and who in many instances had converted to Catholicism and relocated within Canada.

As Iroquois policy unfolded in the first half of the eighteenth century, the League's members sought to maintain their independence and their power by courting both the French and the English and by playing one European power against the other. New York's secretary for Indian affairs wrote in 1750: "To preserve the balance between us and the French is the great ruling principle of modern Indian politics."[11] The Iroquois traded with both of the European powers and accepted lavish gifts from both. They waged war on behalf of neither. The policy of peace was extended to their former Indian adversaries to the north and in the west. This did not mean that the Iroquois abandoned warfare altogether. War remained an important part of their way of life. But their warriors now attacked Indian nations south of Pennsylvania, striking the Cherokees and the Catawbas. Elsewhere, the Iroquois maintained a delicate diplomatic balance intended to keep the peace. The Iroquois Confederation possessed great powers of persuasion, but it never had the authority or the means to coerce individuals. During King George's War (1744–48), some warriors from the Seneca nation in the west fought for the French, while the easternmost nation, the Mohawk, under the influence of William Johnson, provided some assistance to the British. The great majority of Iroquois, however, followed League policy and remained aloof.

Great Britain's claim to the Ohio country rested on the Iroquois deed of 1701. The Iroquois, the English asserted, had conquered the west, and in their renewal of the Covenant Chain had passed their rights of conquest on to the king of England. That claim was suspect. The Iroquois war parties of the previous century had never been large enough, or successful enough, to establish and occupy an inland empire. By 1700, the League no longer had enough warriors to mount an effective military action in the west. Nonetheless, both English authorities and the Iroquois throughout the early eighteenth century carefully cultivated the myth of such an Iroquois empire. With the encouragement of Pennsylvania officials the Iroquois sent viceroys—the English called them "half kings"—to Delaware and Shawnee villages in the Ohio country. The British hoped those "half kings" would help them hold the western Indians in line. But in fact Iroquois did not rule those villages. The "half kings" were really more like ambassadors than governors. As ambitious local chiefs asserted their authority, the representatives of the League could not simply issue orders, but needed to use their powers of persuasion. At one time the "half kings" may have had influence, but in the decade before the outbreak of the Seven Years' War, they lost most of their power.

The villages on the upper Ohio River that the "half kings" pretended to rule had been populated by refugees from the east, displaced by British expansion. In addition to their resentment of Iroquois pretensions, those refugees were angry over the Six Nations' willingness to serve as enforcers for the British. In 1742 the Iroquois had rebuked and threatened Delaware tribesmen who challenged the notorious "Walking Purchase," a forged document used to dispossess them of hundreds of square miles of land in eastern Pennsylvania. Harboring little love for their presumed Iroquois overlords, the newly founded communities in the Ohio country, far from the reach of Iroquois authority, went their own way.

But Iroquois power on the crucial New York frontier was still very much a reality. Alarmed by reports that the Mohawks had repudiated the Covenant Chain after an unsatisfactory meeting with New York Governor George Clinton, the Board of Trade in London in 1753 ordered colonial officials to take steps to win Iroquois support in the coming struggle with France. Representatives of seven of the British colonies met with Iroquois representatives at Albany, New York, in June 1754. Iroquois complaints at the Albany Conference, presented very forcefully by Chief Hendrick

(Theyanoguin) of the Mohawks, tell us much about the difficulties that plagued British relations with prospective Indian allies. British traders, he complained, rather than providing useful goods to Iroquois hunters, sold them too much rum, thereby placing their lives in danger. Hendrick also objected to the activities of British land speculators, who were encroaching upon Iroquois lands in both New York and the west. As to the current conflict with the French over the Ohio country, he declared, "The Governor of Virginia and the Governor of Canada are both quarreling over lands belonging to us and such a quarrel may end in our destruction. They fight to decide who shall have the land."[12] Finally, Hendrick charged that New York had no coherent war policy. Although British agents urged the Iroquois to attack the French, merchants based in Albany sold guns to the French in Canada that would be used to shed Iroquois blood, were they to go to war.

The presiding officer, Lieutenant Governor James De Lancey, protested that those charges were untrue. But ironically, during the conference, representatives of Pennsylvania and Connecticut bought the same tract of land in Pennsylvania's Wyoming valley from corrupt Iroquois chiefs. Although the Iroquois representatives left the Albany Conference laden with British goods given as gifts to win their friendship—some thirty wagon loads, in fact—they remained skeptical of the value of closer ties with Great Britain.

During the French and Indian War, a group of Mohawks who had converted to Catholicism and resettled in Canada supplied warriors to the French army. A pro-British Mohawk faction in New York, under the influence of William Johnson, supported the British war effort in 1755. But after Hendrick was killed that year, while fighting with Johnson against the French, the clan matrons who controlled policy forbade further Mohawk participation. Once again, doubts about Britain's resolution and reliability undercut British efforts to win Iroquois military support. The Mohawks withdrew in 1755; other Iroquois nations generally adhered to the now traditional policy of neutrality throughout most of the war. Only in the last year, when it was clear that French defeat was inevitable, did they abandon neutrality and provide new military aid to the British forces.

After the war, Supreme Commander Lord Jeffrey Amherst's ill-considered seizure of some Iroquois lands to reward his officers aroused new tensions and animosities. A band of Senecas, always the most anti-English of the Iroquois nations, sought support for a Pan-Indian uprising against the victors. Their efforts, although not immediately successful, helped pave the way for the uprisings led by the Ottawa chief Pontiac and others in 1763. But most Iroquois shunned the insurgents. The League was ultimately marginalized as leadership and power in the Indian world shifted to the west.

Case Study 2: The Delaware and Britain's Bid to Control the Ohio Country

If good relations with the Iroquois were essential to English security on the New York frontier, access to the Ohio valley depended upon an accommodation with the Delaware Indians and their close friends and allies, the Shawnee. The Delaware, also called the Lenape, were newcomers to the Ohio country. They had no reason to like or trust the English, for they had been driven from their homelands by land-hungry white settlers and corrupt colonial officials. Loss of Delaware land to white expansionists, which had begun with the removal of Lenape from their villages near the Atlantic coast in the seventeenth century, continued throughout the eighteenth century. The Lenape originally lived in southern New York, New Jersey, Delaware, and eastern Pennsylvania. At the time of first contact with Europeans, they were divided into about forty separate bands speaking two related but distinct Algonquian dialects. Lacking both the strategic location and the unity of the Iroquois, the Delaware were extremely vulnerable.

Although Delaware land rights in Pennsylvania had been recognized and honored by the colony's founder, William Penn, and by the early Quaker settlers, their successors were less principled and more materialistic. Lenape bands in eastern Pennsylvania were forced to relinquish the Tulpehocken and Brandywine valleys, and were resettled in territories on the Susquehanna and its tributaries claimed by the Iroquois and occupied by several other refugee groups. In the Lehigh valley, the Delaware were defrauded and dispossessed by the notorious "Walking Purchase" of 1737, in which speculators associated with Penn's heirs invoked the authority of a fraudulent deed, allegedly given many years earlier to William Penn, to lay claim to some 1,200 square miles of Lenape land. "By 1740," one authority states, "the Delaware had lost most of their own territory, and were forced to live on the lands of their haughty uncles, the Six Nations, or on the lands of equally haughty Europeans. Their condition was pitiful: drunken, disillusioned, dependent, and hostile."[13] Continued pressure from white settlers, sometimes aided and abetted by corrupt Iroquois sachems, combined with the shortage of game and general privation on their remaining eastern lands, impelled many Lenape to leave eastern Pennsylvania. Many found refuge in new communities on the upper Ohio.

Securing an alliance with those western Delaware bands and with tribes closely allied to them was the key to dislodging the French from the Ohio valley. Unfortunately, the supreme commander of British forces in North America in 1755 did not understand that. When Shingas, leader of the western Delaware, asked for a guarantee that the British would not settle on Indian land after they drove out the French, General Braddock told him he had no territorial rights the British needed to respect, because "no savage should inherit land." Shingas warned that Indians would not fight for him unless they were given assurance that they could continue "to live on the land." The general replied that he did not really need Indian help. The British army could easily beat the French.[14] Braddock was mistaken. After his defeat and death near Fort Duquesne, Delaware warriors joined Shawnees, Mingos, Senecas, Cayugas, and Indians from the Illinois country and Great Lakes in attacking English frontier settlements from Pennsylvania south to the Carolinas. Until the Indians made peace in 1758, the backcountry remained unsafe.

The Delaware bands remaining in the east also harbored grievances against the British. Some followed the leadership of Teedyuscung, who in 1755 emerged as the self-styled "King of the Delaware." While the Iroquois and the British both conceded Teedysucung's right to negotiate on behalf of the eastern Lenape, neither recognized his right to reclaim the lands lost in the notorious "Walking Purchase" of 1737. Angered by past injustices and present-day slights, Teedyuscung and his followers would also, for a time, favor the French. However, French failure to provide adequate support for their Native American allies impelled both the western and the eastern Delaware, as well as other Indian belligerents, to make peace with the British before the war's end. That peace, brilliantly brokered by George Croghan and Christian Frederick Post, was grounded in a British promise, soon dishonored, to withdraw from their trans-Appalachian bases and respect Indian land rights in the west.

Case Study 3: The Cherokees, Lost Allies

The Cherokees, whose traditional homelands occupied the interior hill country of the Carolinas and Georgia, had long been important trading partners and allies of the British. Their continued friendship and military support had saved the small, vulnerable Carolina colonies from annihilation in the Yamasee War of 1715. Their relationships with the Carolinians were, nonetheless, often troubled, for disreputable traders cheated and sometimes abused their Cherokee clients. Early in the eighteenth century, some of the leaders of the newly emergent Cherokee confederacy that now sought to coordinate policy among the independent Cherokee towns found it prudent, as a balance against the British, to establish some ties with the French in Louisiana. The Cherokees, much like the Iroquois, were learning to maneuver "in the best tradition of European power politics."[15]

The Cherokees shared one other discovery with the Iroquois: they learned that the British were not reliable allies. The colony of South Carolina had signed a treaty of mutual military aid with the Cherokees, but in 1748, when their Cherokee allies were attacked by the Creeks, the South Carolinians refused to come to their defense. In retaliation, the Cherokees attacked some of the British traders who had abused them, and sent emissaries to the French.

In their preparations for George Washington's campaign against the French in the upper Ohio valley in 1753–54, the Virginia colony asked for Cherokee support. The Cherokees talked of sending a thousand warriors, but sent none. A year later, negotiations for Cherokee assistance to Braddock collapsed as a result of Cherokee anger over trading abuses. The absence of the Cherokees at the forks of the Ohio badly hurt the British.

A small band of Cherokees—probably fewer than 250—served as mercenaries with Virginia frontier forces in 1757–58. When the colony failed to pay them, some of the Cherokee warriors, hungry and footsore on their march home, took food and some stray horses from Virginia settlers. In retaliation, Virginia frontiersmen then began killing other Cherokees returning from military service. They often scalped their victims in order to collect the very large bounty the colony then paid for the hair of enemy Indians. Outraged, in May 1759 Cherokee warriors from the village of Settico retaliated by killing some whites in the backcountry along the Yadkin and Catawba rivers. Soon thereafter a Cherokee war party struck the Carolina frontier, killing twenty settlers. South Carolina cut off trade with the Cherokee nation, and prepared for war.

The British, in the last year of the French and Indian War, were now forced to mount an offensive against a former Indian ally. At first, some Cherokee leaders sought to end the hostilities and restore trade. But when a Cherokee peace delegation journeyed to Charleston, South Carolina's governor, William Henry Lyttelton, ordered them imprisoned as hostages at Fort Prince George. Lyttelton, as a condition for peace and the resumption of trade, demanded that the twenty-four Cherokee warriors who had raided Carolina settlements be turned over for punishment. The Cherokees rejected those terms as too severe, given the British atrocities that had provoked the raids. Negotiations came to an end on January 18, 1760, when Cherokee warriors attacked Fort Prince George and tried to free the hostages. In the fighting, the fort's commander was killed. The garrison's survivors executed all of the members of the Cherokee peace delegation, and drove off the attackers. Cherokee war parties then struck a number of frontier settlements, forcing whites to evacuate most of the Carolina backcountry.

The supreme commander of British military forces in North America, General Jeffrey Amherst, responded to a plea from Governor Lyttelton for assistance against the Cherokees by dispatching 1,600 men under the command of Colonel Archibald Montgomery. After burning several Cherokee villages, and sustaining some casualties in an ambush, Montgomery and his army withdrew.

The Cherokees were not yet pacified. Indeed, after Montgomery's raid, the Cherokee towns, once divided, were united in their determination to renew the war. The killing of the peace delegation had silenced most of the Cherokee advocates of a conciliatory policy toward South Carolina. In the summer of 1760, Cherokee warriors besieged Fort Loudoun in the Cherokee "overhills." After the garrison capitulated, the Cherokees killed twenty-four Carolina soldiers, ostensibly for violating the terms of the surrender by trying to hide some gunpowder. One of the surviving prisoners was tortured to death, some were ransomed, and a few were adopted into the tribe. For a time, it appeared the Cherokees might win, for they drove whites from their hill country homeland. In 1760, South Carolina made no effort to reoccupy the western regions of the colony.

In 1761, however, the British, no longer at war with the French in Canada, sent an army of 2,400 men to punish the Cherokees. They were

assisted by warriors from several tribes historically hostile to the Cherokees: Mohawks, Catawbas, and Chickasaws. The force was commanded
by Lieutenant Colonel James Grant, who refused to accept Cherokee chief
Little Carpenter's offer to surrender in May. Instead, Grant's army burned
fifteen Cherokee towns and destroyed their cornfields, leaving some 5,000
people homeless and hungry. Grant ordered that all Cherokees found in
their villages be killed. Women, children, and the aged as well as warriors
were slaughtered by his troops. One of Grant's men, Lieutenant Francis
Marion (later to win fame as the "Swamp Fox" of the American War for
Independence), was horrified by the brutal treatment of the Indians.
Marion wrote that he "saw everywhere around the footsteps of little Indian children, where they had lately played under the shade of the rustling
corn. When we are gone, thought I, they will return and peeping through
the weeds with tearful eyes, will mark the ghastly ruin where they had so
often played. 'Who did this?' they will ask their mothers and the reply will
be, 'the white people did it—the Christians did it.'"[16]

When Grant finally agreed to peace terms late in the summer of 1761,
he insisted on inclusion of a provision for the execution of four Cherokee
leaders. Through a direct appeal to the Carolina authorities, Little Carpenter was able to secure the withdrawal of that demand. But as the price of
peace, the Cherokees were forced to cede more land and swear allegiance
to the British king.

In the end, the Cherokees stood alone. Cherokee leaders, sensitive
to the need for access to trade, over the years had hoped that through
connection with the French in Louisiana they would find a new source of
the European goods they needed. But in the Anglo-Cherokee War of 1759–
61, the French were unable to offer much help. The Cherokees had also
hoped for support from the Creek Confederacy to the south. Remember-
ing old grievances against the Cherokees, the Creeks remained neutral.
Other Indians, as noted, fought against the Cherokees. Finally, the Cherokees realized that they had no choice but to make the best terms they could
with the victor.

This brief Cherokee case history illustrates several of the major factors that recurred in Anglo-Indian relations throughout the colonial period: the abuse of Indians by lawless whites, the punitive overreactions
of the British to Indian reprisals, the lack of unity among Indian nations
in dealing with the colonies (e.g., the Creek-Cherokee rivalry), the failure of the British to keep their commitments to go to the aid of Indian

military allies, and, finally, the inability of the Indian nations to find a reliable substitute for British trade goods. Running through all the years of
conflict is a deep sense of anger on both sides, an anger expressed on many
occasions in violent acts that in turn generated new violence.

Indians and the Outcome of the War

Great Britain's past relationships with Indian peoples were a liability in the waging of the war against the French in North America. Historical events often have a life of their own that extends far beyond the
lifetimes of the participants, for memories, impressions, and even miscon-
ceptions of the past shape present attitudes and future prospects. The Indians' experiences with British traders and colonists had often been
unfortunate. They had many reasons not to trust the British, and little
inclination to risk their lives for the British empire. The Indian support
that might have paved the way for an early British conquest of New France
was not forthcoming. In the early years of the war, Britain's prospective
allies remained aloof or fought for France. But the Indians were realists.
For the most part, they understood that they could not separate themselves
from Europe; the patterns of dependency were too deeply implanted by
1755. They could not afford to be allied with losers in the European power
struggle. The stakes were too high. With a few exceptions, Indian leaders
sought reliable European trading partners and allies. Great Britain prevailed
in the competition for Indian support not because she had won their affection and trust, but because the Indians concluded late in the war that
she would win.

Notes

1. Wilbur R. Jacobs, ed., *Indians of the Southern Colonial Frontier: The
Edmund Atkin Report and Plan of 1755* (Columbia: University of South Carolina
Press, 1954), 3–4.

2. See, for example, H.R. McIllwaine et al., *Executive Journal of the Colony
of Virginia*, 6 vols. (Richmond: Virginia State Library, 1925–66), 2:351–52, 381–
82, 390, 402, 408. On the trader abuses leading to the Yamasee War, see Verner
W. Crane, *The Southern Frontier 1670–1732* (Ann Arbor: University of Michigan
Press, 1956), 162–82.

3. Quoted in John Buchanan, *Jackson's Way: Andrew Jackson and the People
of the Western Waters* (New York: John Wiley and Sons, 2001), 36.

4. Andrew Jackson to James Monroe, March 4, 1817, in Sam B. Smith and Harriet Chappell Owsley, eds., *The Papers of Andrew Jackson,* 6 vols. (Knoxville: University of Tennessee Press, 1980–2002), 4:95–97.

5. Sir William Johnson to the earl of Dorchester, November 4, 1772, quoted in Richard White, *The Middle Ground: Indians, Empires and Republics in the Great Lakes Region, 1650–1815* (New York: Cambridge University Press, 1991), 315.

6. Clarence E. Carter, ed., *Correspondence of General Thomas Gage with the Secretaries of State, 1763–75,* 2 vols. (New Haven, CT: Yale University Press, 1931), 1:152.

7. Quoted in Nicholas B. Wainwright, *George Croghan: Wilderness Diplomat* (Chapel Hill: University of North Carolina Press, 1959), 232.

8. Quoted in Wiley Sword, *President Washington's Indian War: The Struggle for the Old Northwest 1790–1795* (Norman: University of Oklahoma Press, 1985), 7.

9. James H. Merrell, *Into the American Woods: Negotiators on the Pennsylvania Frontier* (New York: Norton, 1999), 41.

10. Richard Aquila, *The Iroquois Restoration: Iroquois Diplomacy on the Colonial Frontier, 1701–1754* (Lincoln: University of Nebraska Press, 1997), 47.

11. Quoted in Daniel K. Richter, "Native American History: Perspectives on the Eighteenth Century," in *The World Turned Upside-Down: The State of Eighteenth-Century American Studies at the Beginning of the Twenty-first Century,* ed. Michael V. Kennedy and William G. Shade (Bethlehem, PA: Lehigh University Press, 2001), 278.

12. E.B. O'Callaghan and B. Fernow, eds., *Documents Relative to the Colonial History of the State of New York,* 15 vols. (Albany, NY: Weed and Parsons, 1853–87), 6:887.

13. Anthony Wallace, "New Religions Among the Delaware Indians, 1600–1900," *Southwestern Journal of Anthropology* 12 (1956): 4.

14. Beverley W. Bond, Jr., ed., "The Captivity of Charles Stuart," *Mississippi Valley Historical Review* 31 (1926): 63.

15. Gary B. Nash, *Red, White and Black: The Peoples of Early North America,* 4th ed. (Upper Saddle River, NJ: Prentice-Hall, 2000), 232.

16. Quoted in Alan Gallay, ed., *The Colonial Wars of North America, 1512–1763* (New York: Garland, 1996), 123.

Join or Die. This classic cartoon, published in Benjamin Franklin's newspaper to promote the Albany Plan of Union, warned that colonial disunity could mean defeat at the hands of the French. (Library of Congress)

The Burial of General Braddock. This nineteenth-century imaginative re-creation of Braddock's burial memorialized the British defeat near the forks of the Ohio. (Library of Congress)

Louis XV. This French king's inept rule helped pave the way not only for defeat in the Seven Years' War but also for the ultimate collapse of the Old Regime. (Library of Congress)

Louis Joseph, Marquis of Montcalm. Commander of French forces in Canada, this career officer, although later celebrated as a hero and martyr, never mastered the art of waging war in North America. (Library of Congress)

Montcalm Trying to Stop the Massacre. This nineteenth-century imaginative reconstruction portrays Montcalm's unsuccessful effort to stop the killing of British prisoners by Indians at Fort William Henry. (Library of Congress)

William Pitt. Pitt's rise to power in Great Britain led to changes in the management of the war in North America that paved the way for a British victory. (Library of Congress)

Death of General Wolfe. This often reproduced painting by Benjamin West memorialized the battlefield death of the conqueror of Quebec and contributed greatly to the mythology surrounding this battle. (Library of Congress)

George III. The ascent of this young king to the British throne led to a compromise peace with France. His subsequent role in the governing of Great Britain helped inflame relations with the North American colonies. (Library of Congress)

General Jeffrey Amherst. Amherst was a competent if somewhat plodding officer. His insensitive conduct of Indian policy after the war was a major factor in provoking Pontiac's uprising. (Library of Congress)

CHAPTER 5

GREAT BRITAIN'S IMPERIAL CRISIS

In 1758, after returning from two years as a prisoner of war in Canada, a Philadelphia Presbyterian deacon wrote a short book reflecting on his experience that ended with a prediction that the English would lose the war in North America. Even though the French were greatly outnumbered, Robert Eastburn concluded, "They are united as one man, while we may be justly compared to a house divided against itself," a house "that cannot stand long."[1] Eastburn's prediction was wrong, but his perception of colonial disunity was well founded. Each of the British supreme commanders and all of the royal governors could offer numerous examples of colonial squabbling and obstructionism. Great Britain's New World Empire in the 1760s can best be described by a word that was not yet part of the English language: dysfunctional.

Colonial Rivalries Damage the War Effort

British officials and colonial patriots were often frustrated by the refusal of colonial assemblies to provide adequately for the common defense. As it became apparent that war was imminent, colonial governors asked for funds to build or maintain frontier forts. They were often rebuffed. In 1754, the governor of Pennsylvania endorsed a request from Indians at the forks of the Ohio, who asked that the British build a fortified trading post there. The Assembly not only refused to approve the expenditure, but accused the Indian agent George Croghan of fabricating the request. When war broke out a year later, the Pennsylvania Assembly refused to vote any money for frontier defense, even though the colony's western settlements were terrorized by French and Indian raiders after General Edward

Braddock's defeat. Some writers have blamed the Quakers, arguing that as pacifists, Quakers were opposed to war expenditures and, since they generally resided in the east, did not care what happened to non-Quakers in the west. That charge is false. The real reason for the impasse in Pennsylvania lay in a dispute between the popularly elected Assembly and the governor appointed by the proprietors. The Penn family refused to pay any taxes on their extensive landholdings in the colony. The Assembly was not willing to tax others for defense unless the Penns gave up their exemption.

After the situation grew truly desperate, the two parties finally agreed on a compromise whereby the Penns provided a gift of 5,000 pounds to the cause, and the Assembly passed an appropriation of 55,000 pounds "for the King's use."[2] That euphemism was employed to avoid offending the Quakers, who were willing to vote for an appropriation for defense but not to declare war. But the colony remained divided. The Quakers favored peaceful negotiations with the Indians and the restoration of some of the land that had been taken from them. Many Scots-Irish and German settlers demanded an all-out Indian war. Some of the Scots-Irish threatened to march on Philadelphia and overthrow the colonial government if aggressive action was not taken to protect western settlements. Quakers, by contrast, were horrified by some of the measures—such as substantial bounties for the scalps of all enemy Indians over the age of ten—adopted by the colony's new war commission. They responded by withdrawing from Pennsylvania politics, declining to run for reelection to the Assembly. Later in the war, however, prominent Quaker leaders, such as Israel Pemberton, made notable contributions to the negotiations that persuaded the Indians to lay down their arms.

Internal politics also impeded preparations for the defense of New York. The fort at Oswego commanded the approaches to Lake Ontario and served as a major base for the Indian trade. Its importance to the security of the colony cannot be overestimated. But it was in very bad condition on the eve of the war. The New York Assembly, more interested in asserting its authority at the expense of the royal governor than in serving the needs of empire or even the colony's defense, refused to appropriate funds for its maintenance. Governor George Clinton was forced to pay the expenses of Fort Oswego from his own funds. The repairs made were not adequate.

In Virginia, some eastern planters were opposed to the expenditure of public money to protect the interests of western land speculators and settlers. In military appropriations, preference was given to maintaining a powerful militia in the east to prevent slave insurrections. George Washington, in charge of frontier forces, complained that his men lacked the rudimentary supplies of a good army. Some were barefoot. In 1757 manpower shortages forced Washington to abandon eleven of the eighteen forts guarding Virginia's western frontier. With only around 400 men, he could not offer any real protection to those settlers who did not flee eastward. Few remained, in any case. Canada's governor, Pierre Vaudreuil, noted, with some satisfaction, that French and Indian raiding parties "have carried terror among our enemies to a point that the settlements of the English in [the backcountry of] Pensilvanie, Maryland, and Virginia are abandoned. All the settlers have retreated to the cities or into the forest."[3] Rather than responding to Washington's plea for more men, the British commanding general, Lord Loudoun, ordered him to send 200 men to the garrison at Charleston, South Carolina, to guard against a possible slave revolt there.

In Maryland, sectional interests also undercut defense planning. The Assembly, determined to keep spending as low as possible, voted not to defend the western part of the colony. An ongoing struggle between the upper and lower houses blocked efforts to raise troops to fight the French. In the Carolinas, the eastern planters were not directly threatened by the French offensive. Accordingly, they offered little support to the northern colonies or to their own frontier settlers in the early years of the conflict— and, as noted earlier—from 1759 onward were embroiled in a war with the Cherokees.

The one region that made a major commitment from the outset to support the war against the French in Canada was New England. Nathaniel Hawthorne later related that during "the Old French War . . . every man was a soldier, or the father or brother of a soldier, and the whole land literally echoed with the roll of the drum either beating up for recruits among the towns and villages, or striking the march toward the frontiers."[4] It is estimated that around a third of the men of military age in Massachusetts served in the war. Puritan New England, anti-Catholic to the core, harboring dark memories of nearly a century of French and Indian raids, saw this war as a holy crusade. But despite their commitment to victory, New Englanders were not inclined to make sacrifices for the defense of their neighbors in New York. They rejected out of hand New York's appeal for financial aid in constructing and maintaining fortifications on the Canadian frontier. Nor did wartime idealism deter some Boston merchants from enjoying a lucrative, clandestine, and illegal trade with the French in Canada.

Intercolonial rivalries often obstructed the war effort. In 1755, when Massachusetts governor William Shirley succeeded Braddock as supreme commander of British forces in North America, resentful New York politicians employed what Shirley described as "all imaginable obstructions" to prevent him from achieving his objectives.[5] He was undercut not only by the De Lanceys, a powerful New York political family, but also by the Indian agent William Johnson, who refused to supply him with Mohawk scouts. The De Lanceys saw to it that Shirley was denied use of cannons stored at Albany. Shirley's offensive against Fort Niagara, an action that might have paved the way to an early victory over France by cutting water access to the west, had to be abandoned. Shirley's enemies later persuaded London to remove him from command. Johnson also had his detractors. His campaign against Crown Point was marred by friction between New Yorkers and New Englanders, with the latter balking at the decision to employ troops to build a fort for the defense of New York at the south end of Lake Champlain. Fort William Henry was built, but the dissension over its construction tells us much about the disunity that plagued British war efforts.

The territorial aspirations of the individual colonies sometimes drove military planning. Virginians planned through an armed invasion of the west not only to eject the French but also to outflank their Pennsylvania rivals. Colonel Washington's ill-fated march into western Pennsylvania in 1754 was not aimed solely at the French. It was intended to protect Virginia's purported western domain against all comers. Virginia and Pennsylvania were at odds over the Ohio country, which included much of the land in the western part of the future state of Pennsylvania, as well as much of Ohio, Kentucky, and Indiana. Two land companies chartered by Virginia vied for access to the rich meadows and valleys west of the Allegheny Mountains then occupied by the Delaware, the Shawnee, the Miami, the Ottawa, and the Mingo tribes. They planned to persuade the Indians to sell out and move farther west, and then resell the land at great profit to white settlers. In 1755, in order to protect their western interests, Virginians persuaded Braddock to launch his campaign from Virginia, rather than from a more direct staging point in Pennsylvania.

Virginia's promoters were bolstered by a clause in the colony's royal charter that defined the Pacific Ocean as its western boundary. Pennsylvania's proprietors had their own royal charter, however, and they believed that under that more recent grant, the west was theirs. While some Pennsylvanians were land speculators, others profited from trade with the Indians. That trade, primarily in furs, would be destroyed if the land companies removed the Indians and replaced forests with farms and towns. Virginia, Pennsylvania, and New York were unable to agree on measures for the defense of the west. Each feared that its people would be excluded, that the undertaking would benefit some other colony, some other group of investors.

Rejection of the Albany Plan of Union, 1754

Benjamin Franklin of Pennsylvania had foreseen the difficulties the lack of a common colonial military strategy would create in the event of a new war with France. Writing in a Philadelphia newspaper, he warned, "Our enemies have the great advantage of being under one direction, with one Council and one Purse. With Britain so far away, the French can, with impunity, violate the most solemn treaties, kill, seize, and imprison our traders, confiscate our property, murder and scalp our farmers with their wives and children, and take an easy possession of such parts of the British territories as they find most convenient for them: which if they are permitted to do, must end in the destruction of the British interest, trade and plantations in America."[6]

In 1754, Franklin attended the conference at Albany, New York, called at the request of the British Board of Trade for the purpose of reestablishing an alliance with the League of the Iroquois. The conference was not a success. Only seven of the colonies sent commissioners. Virginia was conspicuous by its absence. With the exception of the Mohawks, the Iroquois nations also were poorly represented. Moreover, some of the colonial delegates undercut the purpose of the conference by pursuing secret land deals with Iroquois sachems. The only notable aspect of an otherwise undistinguished gathering was a bold proposal, advanced by

Franklin and endorsed by the conference, to establish a military confederation of colonies in British North America.

Franklin's Plan of Union would have entrusted the defense of the colonies and the conduct of Indian relations to a Union governed by a Grand Council of Delegates representing all of the colonies and headed by a president general appointed by the crown. The colonies would retain their separate governments, which would remain in charge of internal matters. But they would delegate to the Union sole control of Indian affairs. The colonies would no longer negotiate individually with the Indian nations. The Union would regulate Indian trade and land purchases. It would possess the sole right to declare war against an Indian nation or to make peace. In time of war, the Union could levy taxes, raise troops, build forts, construct a navy, and carry out military operations. Delegates stung by Iroquois taunts that the British had proven themselves unable to wage war effectively because of their selfishness and disunity found Franklin's plan attractive.

But Franklin's proposal received little support outside the conference. The project attracted some favorable notice in New England, but none of the colonial assemblies endorsed it. Virginia was strongly opposed, for Virginians had no interest in relinquishing their hopes for western expansion through purchasing Indian land. Other colonies, including New York, Pennsylvania, and Connecticut, harbored similar reservations. The Plan of Union was not looked upon with favor in London, either, for crown officials believed it placed too much authority in the hands of the colonists. The British government preferred to solve the problem of disunity by granting sweeping powers to the supreme commander of British forces in North America. That proved to be unfortunate, for the commanders were not able to exercise those powers in the face of colonial opposition.

Problems of Command: The British Regular Army and the Colonial Militias

In the early years of the French and Indian War, relations between the British army in North America and colonial authorities were often strained. Part of the difficulty can be explained as a reaction to the personal manner and official behavior of one of the supreme commanders. More of that presently. But it must also be noted that a prime cause of the ill feeling and friction that arose between regular British army units and colonial militias was British refusal to respect the rank and status of local commanders. With the resumption of hostilities between the British and the French in North America, military authorities in London, enforcing the terms of the Royal Proclamation of 1754, declared that no colonial militia officer had the right to command in any situation in which an officer of the regular British army was present. That meant that a totally inexperienced and newly commissioned British officer outranked a seasoned colonial militia commander many years his senior. That order hurt the war effort because local militia leaders, many of them veterans of earlier frontier wars, resented their loss of command. Moreover, the Proclamation declared that all troops, whether militia or regular army, were fully subject to British army discipline. Since British courts-martial regularly sentenced minor offenders to severe floggings, and freely employed the death penalty for numerous infractions, this order served as a powerful deterrent to colonial enlistments.

The attitudes of British army officers unfamiliar with warfare in the New World contributed to colonial resentments. Although the French sometimes praised the fighting abilities of the militia (recall, for example, Baron Ludwig Dieskau's tribute to Johnson's men), General James Wolfe expressed the prejudices of many of his colleagues when he declared, in a letter to his wife in 1759, "The Americans are in general the dirtiest, most contemptible cowardly dogs that you can conceive. There is no depending upon them in action. They fall down dead in their own dirt and desert by battalions, officers and all. Such rascals as these are rather an encumbrance than any real strength to an army."[7] Wolfe's comments were both unfair and, aside from a few incidents, factually inaccurate. But they shed some light on one of the sources of the undercurrent of tension that so often impaired the relationships of the British army and the colonial militias.

Massachusetts governor Shirley, during his term as supreme commander of British forces in America, averted conflicts between provincial and royal officers by assigning regulars and colonials to separate units under their own commanders. When John Campbell, the earl of Loudoun, replaced Shirley as supreme commander in 1756, the militia officers assembled at Lake George, New York, sent word that any effort to place them under the command of British regular officers would result in "the dissolution of the army."[8] Loudoun was outraged, for he had a low opinion of militia officers. He blamed his predecessor, Governor Shirley, for the failure to establish proper discipline and deference. But Loudoun was forced to yield the point in order to prevent the massive desertion of New England troops who insisted that the terms of their enlistment exempted them from being placed under the command of officers of the British army. He was horrified to discover that they elected their officers from their own ranks, and would obey only those officers.

Lord Loudoun's Failure and William Pitt's Success

Lord Loudoun came to American armed with a commission that granted him—on paper—unprecedented powers. But his imperious manner offended the American colonists. He failed to win the confidence and trust of either the militia or the colonial legislators. His efforts to exact men and money from the colonial assemblies prompted the assemblies to demand the right to review and approve his specific expenditures. His insistence that local authorities make provision to house his troops met with general resistance. He complained to his superior, the duke of Cumberland, younger son of King George II, that the Americans "have assumed to themselves, what they call Rights and Privileges, totally unknown in the Mother Country . . . for no purpose, but to screen them from giving any aid, of any sort to the Service and refusing us Quarters."[9] His inability to understand the colonists' objections to his authoritarian ways foreshadowed the misunderstandings that would lead in the next decade to the American Revolution.

Loudoun on occasion forced private citizens to provide lodging for soldiers in their homes. The troops were generally not welcome, for colonists resented the intrusion and the expense that practice entailed. The discovery that many of those soldiers were infected with smallpox led to further ill feelings. With much grumbling, officials in New York and Philadelphia arranged for public accommodations for some of Loudoun's troops. In Philadelphia, the barracks could house only about half of his men. Throughout much of the winter of 1756–57 some of the rest slept on the ground in unheated sheds or stables. A number died from exposure. In addition to the quartering controversy, Loudoun was soon involved in a dispute with the New England colonial assemblies over the question of who had the right to set quotas for the raising of troops. His high-handed insistence that the assemblies were not to be consulted in the matter antagonized even the royal governors. Thomas Pownall, governor of Massachusetts, supported the assembly in its defiance of Loudoun's orders.

During Loudoun's tour of duty, resistance to service in the regular army became so acute that anti-recruitment riots broke out in four colonies in 1757. In one town in New Hampshire, Loudoun's agents were not only chased out of town, but pursued for some four miles. Those riots did not signify lack of support for the war against the French. Militia enlistment in New England in 1757 soared after the French attack on Fort William Henry. But colonists resented Loudoun's pretensions, and saw in his behavior a threat to their rights and liberties. Loudoun, too, was resentful, complaining to one correspondent that he had "an Eternal Negotiation to carry on" and every day encountered "all sorts of opposition."[10]

In December 1757, the head of the British government, William Pitt, recalled Loudoun. Pitt was determined to conquer Canada. While he was willing to make a major commitment of British troops to achieve that objective, he realized that much of the fighting would have to be done by colonial militia. Colonial morale was therefore of the utmost importance. Loudoun's bad relationships with militia leaders were thus a serious liability. Pitt also understood that Loudoun's efforts to coerce the colonial assemblies and governors had backfired. Rather than giving the new military commander, General James Abercromby, the authority that Loudoun had possessed to demand resources from the colonies, Pitt restored the old prerogatives of the governors and the colonial assemblies. He offered them financial subsidies to help pay for the war effort. Pitt also reversed the policy of downgrading colonial militia officers who served with regular troops. Henceforth, provincials who held the rank of major or above would outrank British officers of lower rank. Pitt's reforms revitalized the war effort in North America. Militia enlistments added 23,000 new men to the British forces within a month after word reached the colonies of Pitt's offer of aid.[11] Some colonial assemblies made major sacrifices to pay for the war. Overall, the colonials, through taxation and borrowing, raised 60 percent of the costs of the conflict in North America. But the financial contributions of some of the colonies were negligible.

Paying for Imperial Defense

The Seven Years' War placed a great burden on the British people. Taxes were high; the war debt, enormous. The refusal of some of the colonial assemblies to raise the war funds Loudoun demanded, or to provide more generous support after his recall, angered many British officials. Those officials were prone to ignore the contributions of the Americans who responded handsomely to Pitt's initiatives; they focused instead on the problems of Braddock and Loudoun early in the war. When George Croghan visited the Board of Trade in London in 1764 (a year after the war was officially over), he discovered that the "chief study of the people in power here at present is to lay heavy taxes on the colonies." He predicted that in its next session Parliament would impose "an internal tax" on the Americans. British officials, Croghan concluded, were "immensely ignorant."[12]

Croghan's observations were prophetic. In 1765, with little dissent, Parliament passed the Stamp Act. Under its provisions colonists were now required to pay a direct tax, by buying a revenue stamp, on all legal documents, commercial papers, newspapers, almanacs, pamphlets, dice, and cards. In addition to this unprecedented direct internal taxation on those domestic transactions, Parliament sought to raise additional funds through the Sugar Act of 1764. That law lowered duties on imported molasses (used by the colonists to make rum), raised duties on a number of other imported products, and granted sweeping new power to the royal officials charged with the suppression of colonial smuggling. Colonists accustomed to easy evasion of the older laws regulating their overseas commerce were outraged.

Together, the Stamp Act and the Sugar Act would raise only about half the money needed to maintain the garrisons in North America that the British government believed were needed to defend the colonies from Indian attack or foreign aggression. Since the British government would still be providing a heavy subsidy to pay for the military establishment in the colonies, most members of Parliament and all the king's ministers believed those measures were eminently reasonable.

Benjamin Franklin and several other colonial agents residing in London tried to tell them that they were mistaken. They advised Prime Minister Sir George Grenville that the colonists, being unrepresented in Parliament, would never accept direct taxation by Parliament. They believed that British subjects could be legally taxed only with their consent. But Grenville and his colleagues were unwilling to accept their advice that reliance be placed once again on the colonial assemblies to raise money for defense. The colonists, in their view, simply could not be trusted to pay their fair share. They must therefore be coerced. The British made no effort to resolve imperial problems through consultation, compromise, and cooperation. Grenville and his colleagues were convinced that the steps they were taking to tax the North American colonies and regulate their trade were essential to reform and strengthen the administration of the empire.

Who Ruled the British Colonies?

At the root of the controversy between colonies and mother country that would soon unfold was a basic disagreement over the nature of the empire and over the question of who had the right to tax. Many colonists, accustomed to enjoying quasi-independence during the long period of "salutary neglect" when England had essentially left the colonies alone, believed that they were not subject to the direct legislative authority of Parliament. In their view, they owed allegiance to the king, but could be taxed only by their own elected colonial assemblies. The British government, by contrast, insisted that Parliament could legislate directly for the colonies. The fact that it had not done so regularly in no way suggested that it did not have the right to do so when the needs of the empire required it. Moreover, critics of colonial claims argued that British subjects overseas, although not directly represented in Parliament, did enjoy "virtual representation" through members of Parliament, who, although elected by districts in the home islands, looked after the interests of all British subjects.

George Croghan's characterization of British policy makers as "immensely ignorant" was extreme, but his reservations about their understanding of America were not unwarranted. Both the Parliament and the king's ministers seem not to have understood that they did not in fact enjoy the unquestioned power to rule in Boston, New York, Charleston, and elsewhere in the colonies that they were accustomed to wield in the cities and villages of the home islands. The Stamp Act was unenforceable. The public protests and mob violence that greeted efforts to apply the law in the colonies came as a great shock. But Britain's rulers had to face the fact that after the first riots, no one would serve as a stamp seller in America, for such people faced tarring and feathering at the very least. In confusion and disbelief, the British abandoned that particular effort to make colonists help pay for the costs of maintaining a British military establishment in North America.

There is not space in this book to describe the various attempts of the British government over the next decade to work out some means of resolving the imperial crisis. Suffice it to say that the American Revolution, which was by no means inevitable, reflected not only the failure of Britain's ruling elite to devise a rational system of imperial administration, but also its astounding inability to deal with British subjects in the American colonies in a flexible, sensitive manner. The rigid, authoritarian, and condescending style so vividly exemplified in the North American careers of General Braddock and Lord Loudoun were often matched by King George III and his ministers in the two decades between Britain's triumph on the Plains of Abraham and the loss of her North American colonies. General Cornwallis's surrender to General Washington and his ragtag army in 1781 ended the debate over whether Parliament could legislate for this particular part of the empire. During the ceremony, the band played a tune called "The World Turned Upside Down." Ironically, Washington's victory was made possible by aid from the same nation that Washington had fought in the previous war. American independence represented many things, but the French might well regard it as their revenge for Montcalm's defeat.

Notes

1. Robert Eastburn, *A Faithful Narrative, of the Many Dangers and Sufferings as well as Wonderful and Surprizing Deliverances of Robert Eastburn, During His Late Captivity Among the Indians* (Philadelphia: William Dunlap, 1758), 38.

2. Fred Anderson, *Crucible of War* (New York: Alfred A. Knopf, 2000), 161.

3. Quoted in Sylvester K. Stevens and Donald H. Kent, *Wilderness Chronicles of North-Western Pennsylvania* (Harrisburg: Commonwealth of Pennsylvania, 1941), 109–10.

4. Quoted in Fred Anderson, *A People's Army: Massachusetts Soldiers and Society in the Seven Years' War* (Chapel Hill: University of North Carolina Press, 1984), 61.

5. Quoted in John Schutz, *William Shirley: King's Governor of Massachusetts* (Chapel Hill: University of North Carolina Press, 1961), 201.

6. *Pennsylvania Gazette,* May 9, 1754.

7. Quoted in Noel St. John Williams, *Redcoats Along the Hudson* (London: Brassy's, 1998), 159–60.

8. Quoted in Anderson, *Crucible of War,* 145.

9. Stanley M. Pargellis, ed., *Military Affairs in North America, 1748–1765: Selected Documents from the Cumberland Papers in Windsor Castle* (New York: Appleton-Century, 1936), 230.

10. Quoted in Anderson, *Crucible of War,* 210.

11. Ibid., 277.

12. Quoted in Nicholas B. Wainwright, *George Croghan: Wilderness Diplomat* (Chapel Hill: University of North Carolina Press, 1959), 206.

CHAPTER 6

AFTER THE WAR

At the close of the Seven Years' War, John Carteret, first earl of Granville, a prominent politician close to King George III, declared it "the most glorious war and the most triumphant peace that England has ever known."[1] Neither Granville, who died shortly after the signing of the Peace of Paris in 1763, nor his colleagues could foresee that Britain's great triumph would set the stage for the loss of most of her North American colonies in the following decade. With France removed as a threat to the northern colonies, and with Spain displaced from Florida and placed in weak control of Louisiana, Britain's colonists had little to fear from European enemies. They were thus less inclined to tolerate what some regarded as British tyranny.

This new mood of defiance was expressed not only in the well-known resistance to parliamentary taxation and regulation, but also in mob violence against unpopular British agents. Particular targets were naval recruiters and their press-gangs, which sometimes kidnapped men off the streets of seaport towns and forced them into service in the Royal Navy. Conditions in the naval service were horrible: bad food, backbreaking work, and brutal discipline. Many victims of impressment did not survive the first year. Anti-impressment riots broke out in Newport, Rhode Island, in 1765, 1769, and 1772; in Wilmington, North Carolina, in 1769; and in New York City in 1775. Although those incidents are not often remembered, having been overshadowed by greater events such as the Boston Tea Party, they were a clear indication of trouble to come. It is telling that British authorities were so insensitive to the feelings of their American subjects that they believed a brutal practice barely tolerated in the slums of London could be used with impunity in the New World. After 1763, Britain's prestige and power in America waned. In a new Treaty of Paris in 1783, she acknowledged the loss of the colonies that made up the newly independent United States.

For France, the consequences of the Seven Years' War are somewhat less obvious, but they were nonetheless profound. To understand the postwar impact of France's defeat, we must first look at her management of diplomatic and military affairs in the 1750s. The French government did not anticipate that occupation of contested territories in the Ohio and St. Lawrence watersheds and in Acadia (Nova Scotia) would lead to a sustained and successful British attack on Canada, let alone to a worldwide war. In fact, neither side in 1754 intended or foresaw the Seven Years' War. Perhaps if power relationships in Europe had been stable, the conflict could have been localized on the American continent and remained an undeclared and low-grade war. But Europe was not stable. A diplomatic revolution realigned Prussia, formerly a French ally, with Great Britain, while Austria, hitherto France's adversary, won French support for her diplomatic and military offensive against Frederick the Great of Prussia by way of an ostensibly defensive alliance. After the outbreak of war between Prussia and Austria, French troops were committed to Empress Maria Theresa's campaign to retake Silesia from the Prussians. France's national security was not at stake, but some of the advisers of Louis XV believed that her influence in central Europe was. France would pay a high price to maintain what proved to be a mere illusion of control, for Austria's able foreign minister, Prince Wenzel von Kaunitz, emerged as the master manipulator of the Franco-Austrian alliance.

Since Prussia was a smaller state, without major continental allies, the French and the Austrians foresaw a short conflict and an easy victory. It was not to be. Prussia, now allied with, and subsidized by, her former enemy Great Britain, was led by one of history's greatest, and luckiest, military leaders, King Frederick the Great. It was a source of great humiliation to France and Austria that even with the support of Russia (withdrawn after the death of Empress Elizabeth in 1762), the Austro-French war against Frederick ended indecisively. The cost in lives and treasure had been staggering.

It must be emphasized again that French involvement in the German war was not necessary to the achievement of rational diplomatic objectives. The historian Walter Dorn comments: "Nothing can be more firmly established today than the fact that France on the eve of the Seven Years' War was not compelled to choose between Austria and Prussia. A firm, clear-sighted direction of foreign affairs could have obtained Austrian neutrality without completely breaking with Prussia."[2] It should have been obvious to all that France could not simultaneously fight an overseas war against British colonies and a continental war without incurring great expense and running great risks. The war in central Europe, although far less crucial to France's real interests than the overseas imperial struggle, claimed the lion's share of French energy and resources. When an able, newly appointed foreign minister, the duke of Choiseul, sought in 1759 to allocate resources from the German war to the more crucial overseas conflict with Great Britain, it was already too late, for France had lost control of the sea-lanes.

Throughout most of the 1750s, France's government was not in the hands of competent planners. Choiseul, a man of intelligence and energy, was an exception. Preoccupation with British imperial blundering must not lead us to overlook the situation in Paris. One historian remarks: "One cannot even say that 'miscalculation' accounted for France's having ended up fighting, to borrow a modern expression, the wrong war, at the wrong time, in the wrong place. It did so because it basically did not calculate at all. During the early 1750's, there was no real 'government in France,' if by that term we mean a centrally directed organization having a settled national purpose."[3] The lazy, inept, and debauched Louis XV reigned but did not rule. Timid and insecure, he had little talent for decision-making, and lacked any real grasp of public affairs. Nonetheless, after the death of Cardinal Andre Fleury in 1743, the king refused to appoint a prime minister. The bureaucracy that made decisions within narrow departmental confines was, with a very few notable exceptions, mediocre and inefficient. The able seldom remained long in office, and there was little coordination among departments.

The most powerful member of the royal court in the 1750s was the king's former mistress Madame de Pompadour, a woman who, some said, judged everything in terms of her personal needs and therefore "had a childish view of the French national interest."[4] One foreign minister, after leaving the king's service, wrote of "open war between the Navy and Army ministers; the men in office unfit for their work and the public have no confidence in them; scandalous extravagance at Court; the people in a state of misery, no patriotism. Madame de Pompadour controls the government with the caprices of an infant, while the King looks blandly on, undisturbed by our worries, and indifferent to public embarrassments."[5] Given her reputation, it is not surprising that Austrians seeking support for the Silesian reannexation lobbied Pompadour. France's king, armed with power he had neither the talent nor the inclination to use to advantage, was no match for Britain's William Pitt or for Prussia's Frederick the Great. Both were men of exceptional insight and audacity. When at war's end Louis XV was memorialized in a huge statute representing him as a victorious warrior astride a great horse, some Parisians snickered. Others bowed their heads in shame.

France's defeat in the Seven Years' War did not cause the French Revolution, which began in 1789, but it did much to expose corruption and incompetence in the Old Regime and thereby hasten the cataclysm. A particularly intractable problem was the staggering war debt, which strained a corrupt, unfair, and inefficient system of tax collection. Interest on the debt alone now consumed some 60 percent of the treasury's revenues.[6] That burden might have been bearable had the regime followed a consistently cautious and frugal policy. But two decades after the end of the Seven Years' War, expenditures in support of American independence plunged the nation into a severe fiscal crisis. However satisfying Great Britain's humiliation may have been, France could not afford that adventure: "91% of the monies needed for the American war came from loans."[7] Although the British government under Pitt and his successors had raised new taxes to meet an equally oppressive debt burden incurred during the Seven Years' War and afterward, the French, burdened with a less efficient and more corrupt tax collection system, were not able to raise sufficient funds from tax revenues to cover current obligations. By 1787, the government could no longer find lenders willing to advance credit to cover the deficit. Several prominent financiers who had previously lent to the government were now bankrupt.[8]

Earlier, two ministers of finance intent on fiscal reform—Anne-Robert Turgot and Jacques Necker—had been forced from office by the opposition of aristocratic vested interests. But now Charles-Alexandre de Calonne, Louis XVI's new finance minister, warned the king "that fiscal reform was absolutely necessary." In fact, the need for such reform had long been obvious. Not only was the tax collection system inefficient, it was manifestly unfair. While the exactions of tax collectors fell heavily on those least able to pay, they also vexed the prosperous middle class by their inequities, for the nobility (who composed only about 8 percent of the state) enjoyed exemptions resented by the masses. The peasantry bore the heaviest burdens. "Under the Old Regime," one noted French historian declared with only slight exaggeration, "the richer a man was, the less he paid."[9] Another scholar added that the need to increase taxes to service the war debt and pay for the military establishment that supported France's claim to great power status came at a time when the poor faced particular hardships: "In the later decades of the eighteenth century, an economic depression and rapid rise in some prices intensified pauperization and destitution. Under such circumstances, increased taxes were not just a burden, they became an oppression. Resentment over increased taxation inflamed public opinion and easily turned into political conflict."[10]

The inability of the Old Regime to deal with the fiscal crisis through a rational and equitable reform of the tax system is on virtually every historian's list of the causes of the French Revolution. "The end of the Old Regime," wrote one historian, "was brought about in the first instance by a cash flow crisis."[11] The privileged refused to cooperate with the monarchy in resolving the problem, and won support from the judiciary, forcing an appeal to the nation. In summoning the Estates General, a popular assembly that had not met in several centuries, Louis XVI intended only to seek fiscal assistance. But the meetings of the Estates General in 1789 gave voice to the anger and frustration of the Third Estate, composed of businessmen, professionals, intellectuals, and untitled landowners, as well as peasants and workers. Led by representatives from the more affluent middle-class interests supported by a few members of the nobility and clergy, the spokesmen of the Third Estate demanded reforms that would severely limit the privileges of the First Estate (nobility) and Second Estate (clergy). Those demands won broad popular support and forced some constitutional concessions from a reluctant king. As rumors spread of an aristocratic conspiracy against popular liberty (the Great Fear), revolutionary forces mobilized and pressed further reform demands through mob action. Even so, an astute monarch might well have managed a reasonably peaceful transition to a limited constitutional monarchy. But Louis XVI, while more dutiful than his grandfather, lacked wisdom and tact. His actions, sometimes hesitant, sometimes rash, rarely politic, and ultimately reactionary, played a key role in unleashing forces that brought down both the monarchy and the aristocracy. We cannot relate the history of the French Revolution in these pages. We must, however, stress the close relationship between the unresolved fiscal problems exacerbated by the Seven Years' War and the coming of revolution in 1789.

Let us return now to North America. Few Native Americans could foresee all of the long-range effects on their lives of the British victory, but many were uneasy. British bungling led to renewed Indian warfare in 1763. The new war can be traced directly to the blunders of Great Britain's supreme military commander in North America. Lord Jeffrey Amherst refused to listen to the advice of seasoned agents and traders on matters of Indian policy. Over the objections of Sir William Johnson, George Croghan, and others wise in the ways of the frontier, Amherst curtailed the long-standing practice of giving gifts of trade goods to friendly tribes each year. Indians regarded gift giving as a means of confirming alliances; Amherst's refusal to continue the practice symbolized hostility and suggested that war was imminent. Amherst also raised the price of trade goods and restricted their sale to a few well-controlled distribution points. This brought hardship and suffering to Indian villages, for their hunters were dependent on access to guns, powder, and shot, now very hard to get. Finally, Amherst, as noted earlier, took land from the Iroquois and awarded it to some of his favorite officers.

In 1763, Indian uprisings against the British set the western frontier ablaze. The best known of the leaders of that insurgency was the Ottawa chief Pontiac. Although this Indian war is often called the Conspiracy of Pontiac, the Ottawa warrior was only one of several independent local chiefs involved in the uprising. The movement had no single leader. Many of those who participated, however, were inspired by the teachings of a Delaware Indian holy man named Neolin. Pontiac often told insurgent warriors and fellow war chiefs the story of Neolin's visit to the Great Spirit. Inspired by a dream to visit heaven, and treated as an honored guest after he arrived there at the end of a long and hard trek, Neolin, as Pontiac related the story, had learned from the lips of the Creator that whites were evil people created not by God but by a malevolent spirit. The Creator revealed that he had punished his Indian children because of their involvement with those evil people. They had offended the Creator by surrendering to whites land he intended only for Indians. They had coveted the white man's goods, drunk his alcohol, and imitated his greedy ways. In punishment the Great Spirit had sent away the game and allowed his true people to live in misery. But now, if they would repent, return to their old ways, share with one another, and give up alcohol and trade goods, he would restore the world they had lost. Not only would the game return and submit to being taken by the bow and arrow, but the Great Spirit himself would assist in ridding the land of the white man. "Drive them out," the Great Spirit told the prophet. "Make war upon them, I do not love them at all, they know me not, and are my enemies."[12]

Pontiac and other Indian leaders who led uprisings in 1763 were determined to drive all white settlers from the west. Their warriors came from a number of tribes, some of them former adversaries now united in opposition to white expansionism. Many, including Pontiac, hoped for the return of the French and exempted them from the condemnation of whites as the spawn of the Evil One. The French, few in number, had proven themselves good trading partners who did not threaten to drive them from their lands. The success of the uprising depended on obtaining gunpowder, shot, and other supplies from a European ally. But frontier rumors notwithstanding, the king of France was in no position, and had little inclination, to reclaim his North American empire. The French traders who remained in the west offered only limited aid.

The British military commander in North America, Lord Amherst, called for the capture and execution of the Indians responsible for the 1763 uprising. His order could not be carried out. The insurgents were too powerful, and by the summer of 1763 controlled most of the Ohio country and the upper Great Lakes region. Pontiac and other raiders terrorized the frontier and burned a number of smaller military outposts. However, they failed to take the three major frontier forts: Detroit, Fort Pitt (formerly Fort Duquesne, at the forks of the Ohio), and Niagara. All three were short of supplies and close to capitulation when, late in the year, the Indians broke off the sieges and returned to their villages to conduct the winter hunt. The Indian war in 1763 ended in a stalemate.

In the following year, the recall of Amherst made it possible for field officers and Indian agents to balance a new military offensive with offers of a generous negotiated peace. Short of supplies and in need of trade goods, many of the belligerents were now willing to settle. In early 1765, Pontiac himself agreed to peace terms, and promised to use his influence to persuade others. A few bands continued hostilities for several months thereafter, but Pontiac's War finally ended on terms very different from those contemplated by Amherst. None of the leaders were executed. In exchange for their promise to keep the peace, restore all captives, and protect the traders in their midst, the formerly rebellious tribes were given great quantities of the gifts Amherst had determined to deny them.

Pontiac's rebellion reinforced reservations in London about the costs of western expansion and prompted a reassessment of Indian policy. Although the crown had designated two superintendents of Indian affairs, for the northern and southern colonies, respectively, those officers were not able to prevent the abuse of Indians by speculators, land companies, and squatters. To avert the outbreak of Indian wars that would sap the empire's resources, policy makers in London decided to establish in the west a large reserve closed to white settlement. The Proclamation of 1763 declared that until the crown negotiated new treaties with the Indian nations, no whites were permitted to reside west of a line running along the crest of the Appalachian Mountains. Those whites currently living in the forbidden territories were to evacuate their settlements immediately. The Proclamation declared that in the future neither colonies nor private individuals would be permitted to negotiate with Indians or buy land from them. Those who traded with Indians were now required to be licensed by the crown and to post a bond to guarantee compliance with crown regulations. The British government did not intend to block western settlement permanently, but hoped to provide for orderly, peaceful expansion. Pontiac's rebellion underscored the dangers of dealing too roughly with the Indian nations.

The policy embodied in the Proclamation of 1763 failed, not only because frontiersmen defied authority and colonial governments resented the loss of their prerogatives, but also because the crown's own agents were often in collusion with those who sought to dispossess Indians in order to serve the short-term interests of land speculators. The Treaty of Fort Stanwix of 1768 is a case in point. The negotiators were not content to obtain from the Iroquois rights to settle in western Pennsylvania and portions of western Virginia and eastern Ohio; they also bought Kentucky from the Six Nations chiefs. The Iroquois had no rightful claim to Kentucky; the Shawnees claimed it as a hunting preserve, and the Cherokees also had some claims there. Kentucky had never been Iroquois, but it was much coveted by several land companies that were quite willing to exploit the fictitious Iroquois claim.

Shawnee efforts to assert their rights in Kentucky through peaceful means proved unavailing as whites claimed the land as their own under the pretext that the Iroquois sale was legitimate and binding. Kentucky soon was "the dark and bloody ground," a theater of racial warfare as attacks on white settlers prompted retaliatory attacks on Indians. The role played by Virginia's royal governor, Lord Dunmore, illustrates the failure of British Indian policy. In 1774, a number of peaceful Indians, including some Shawnees, were butchered by white homesteaders in two massacres on the Ohio River near Wheeling, West Virginia. Although the local Shawnee chief, Cornstalk, tried to avert war, another chief, Logan (a man of Mingo and Shawnee ancestry), who had lost his family in the killings, led a retaliatory raid on white settlements. Governor Dunmore was well aware of the circumstances. The whites who killed Logan's family, he wrote, displayed "an extraordinary degree of cruelty and inhumanity."[13] But when Virginia's agent at Pittsburgh spread a rumor that all the Shawnees were now at war with the British, Dunmore yielded to pressure and sent an army to plunder and burn the Shawnee villages in Ohio. One historian, who characterizes Lord Dunmore's War as a "brief orgy of irresponsibility, cruelty and despair," has concluded that the governor, in collusion with speculators, used the incident as a pretext for "taking Indian land."[14] As to the broader policy issue of protecting Indians from white aggression, Governor Dunmore advised his superiors in London that the Proclamation of 1763 was unenforceable.

But George III's ministers still hoped to avert conflict with Indian nations by closing the frontier. In June 1774, Parliament passed the Quebec Act. One of the pieces of imperial legislation American revolutionaries called the Intolerable Acts, the law provided for the protection of the Roman Catholic Church and the continuation of French civil law in Quebec. While that aspect of the Quebec Act offended Protestant militants in New England and elsewhere, the law angered land speculators even more by extending the boundaries of Quebec to incorporate the northwest from the Ohio River on the south to the Mississippi on the west, thus thwarting the aspirations of colonies that hoped to annex Indian lands in the west. The absence in the Quebec Act of any provision for a popularly elected assembly or for protection of the customary "rights of Englishmen" provided fuel for revolutionary propagandists, who warned that Great Britain now threatened to destroy liberty in North America.

With the outbreak of the American Revolution, most Indian nations either tried to remain neutral or supported the British cause. The British showed them little gratitude, and made no real effort to protect their interests in the treaty ending the Revolutionary War. When the American colonies gained their independence, the Native American peoples faced an aggressive expansionist power that had little regard for Indian rights.

At first the new republic claimed that Indians were a conquered people whose lands now belonged to the United States of America. But in fact the Indian nations of the Ohio and Mississippi valleys had never been defeated by American troops. Nor did the impoverished and weak government established under the Articles of Confederation have the military means to take the land by force. There followed a period in which the United States sought to negotiate land cession treaties with the various Indian nations. In New York, the once proud Iroquois either sought refuge in Canada or were crowded into narrow tracts of land one historian has described as "slums in the wilderness."[15] When Indian nations in the northwest refused to give up the land that whites coveted, it was frequently occupied by white squatters. Neither the states nor the national government possessed the ability or, it must be said, the inclination to protect Indian lands from such encroachments. But when Indians attacked the white interlopers, often in response to violence initiated by the settlers, the United States waged war against the Indians.

In the late 1780s several Indian nations in the Old Northwest resolved that they would permit no white settlement north of the Ohio River. Led by the Shawnee chief Blue Jacket and the Miami chief Little Turtle, they formed an Indian confederacy that defeated the United States army in 1791 and 1792. In the latter engagement, forces under General Arthur St. Clair sustained the highest percentage casualty rate (over 60 percent killed or wounded) ever suffered by an army of the United States. In 1794, however, General Anthony (Mad Anthony) Wayne defeated the Indian confederation in the battle of Fallen Timbers near the modern city of Toledo, Ohio. Wayne understood Indian weaknesses, and exploited their inability to conduct a prolonged war. Although many Indian fighters had survived Fallen Timbers, Wayne's scorched earth policy—burning Indian villages and food supplies—forced the Indians to surrender. In the treaty of Greenville (1795), they ceded most of Ohio to the United States. White settlers quickly occupied the new acquired territory, which was granted statehood just eight years later.

After Fallen Timbers, Blue Jacket and Little Turtle had looked for help from a British fort, built on American territory only a few miles from the battlefield at Fallen Timbers. The British had refused to evacuate a number of forts on American soil in the Old Northwest, justifying that action by pointing to certain American violations of the peace treaty, including nonpayment of pre-Revolution debts owed to British merchants. Their agents had given some encouragement to Indians who spoke of resisting American expansionism. But Great Britain did not want war with the United States. The British commandant at Fort Miami, understanding the limits of British policy, therefore slammed shut the gates to the fort and ignored the warriors' pleas. Once again Britain had misled and betrayed her Indian friends.

Twenty years later, Indians hoping to preserve their territorial integrity from Euro-American aggression would again look to the British for aid. Once again, the outcome would be bitter. In the company of kinsmen who had no desire to live in the shadow of the new American settlements, after Fallen Timbers the young Shawnee warrior Tecumseh Timbers had built a new community in Indiana in a region still unoccupied by whites. Inspired by the religious vision of his younger brother Lalawethika, later known as Tenskwatawa or the Shawnee Prophet, Tecumseh and other followers of the Prophet returned to Ohio in 1804. At the settlement they established near the ruins of Wayne's old fort at Greenville, Tenkswatawa preached a gospel of Native American unity and cultural renewal to visitors from Indian communities throughout the Old Northwest. Opposed by a rival band of Shawnees and by most Ohio whites, Tecumseh and the Prophet in 1807 returned to Indiana and on the Tippecanoe River built a sacred community whites named Prophetstown. There they attracted hundreds of Indians from many tribes, all committed to following the Prophet's teachings.

In 1809 the territorial governor, William Henry Harrison, obtained a new treaty from compliant and corrupt chiefs that gave the United States title to a vast tract of new land in Indiana. Tecumseh and the Prophet sought to rally Indian opposition to the treaty. They hoped to forge a great

new Indian confederation, stretching from the Gulf of Mexico to the Great
Lakes and encompassing Indians of the western plains as well. Their confederation alone, Tecumseh declared, had the right to sell land. Most Indians in the northwest rejected his claim to authority. Governor Harrison
knew full well that the Prophet and Tecumseh did not have the means to
mount an all-out war, but he feared that their agitation would make Indiana unattractive to white settlers. Accordingly, in 1811 Harrison's troops
attacked and burned Prophetstown. The brothers sought aid from the
British in Canada, and received some supplies and some guarded encouragement. When war broke out between the United States and Great Britain in 1812, Tecumseh and warriors he recruited from many tribes fought
in support of the British. However, despite Tecumseh's pleas, the British
army decided to abandon the west in 1813. Tecumseh, refusing to retreat,
died that year in the battle of the Thames in the modern province of
Ontario, near the American city of Detroit, which he had helped capture
early in the war. Far to the south, Andrew Jackson, with the aid of Indians who chose to ally themselves to the United States, suppressed the Red
Stick movement, an uprising led by Creeks who drew some of their in-
spiration from Tecumseh and the Prophet.

After the war of 1812, General Jackson, negotiating on behalf of
the United States, forced both his Indian allies and his former Indian adversaries to give up vast portions of their tribal lands in the southeast.
Elected to the presidency in 1828, Jackson embarked upon an aggressive program of Indian removal through the negotiation of treaties providing for relocation of the eastern Indian nations to territory west of
the Mississippi. Although removal was technically voluntary, Jackson and
his associates made it clear that Indians who resisted would not be protected by the United States, and would be at the mercy of the states and
the local white populations. Of the hundreds of thousands of Indians
who had inhabited the Ohio and Mississippi valleys, the deep south, and
the frontier regions of all of Britain's colonies in 1760, only a handful,
numbering no more than 10,000, remained east of the Mississippi River
eighty years later.

It can be argued that there were no real victors in the Seven Years'
War. For Great Britain, postwar measures intended to provide rational
order in imperial administration and raise funds for the common defense
were conceived and executed in ways that offended colonial feelings and

injured colonial interests. They provoked a revolution that ended in American independence. In France, a fiscal crisis made acute by a huge war debt exposed the inability of the Old Regime to resolve internal conflicts and tensions, and helped bring about the French Revolution of 1789. For Native Americans, the war's outcome hastened their dispossession. The Trail of Tears was part of a process that had many beginnings. One of those beginnings may be traced to that morning in 1754 when Virginia militiamen fired on a small French detachment near the forks of the Ohio.

Notes

1. Quoted in Francis B. Parkman, *Montcalm and Wolfe* (New York: Da Capo Press, 1995), 544.

2. Walter L. Dorn, *Competition for Empire, 1740–1763* (New York: Harper Torchbooks, 1963), 307.

3. Frank W. Brecher, *Losing a Continent* (Westport, CT: Greenwood Press, 1998), 157.

4. Ibid., 7.

5. Abbe de Bernis, quoted in Noel St. John Williams, *Redcoats Along the Hudson* (London: Brassy's 1998), 32.

6. James C. Riley, *The Seven Years' War and the Old Regime in France* (Princeton, NJ: Princeton University Press, 1986), 192, 231.

7. Simon Schama, *Citizens: A Chronicle of the French Revolution* (New York: Alfred A. Knopf, 1989), 61.

8. Orville T. Murphy, *The Diplomatic Retreat of France and Public Opinion on the Eve of the French Revolution, 1783–1789* (Washington, DC: Catholic University of America Press, 1998), 39.

9. Georges Lefebvre, *The Coming of the French Revolution*, trans. R.R. Palmer (Princeton, NJ: Princeton University Press, 1989), 21, 23.

10. Murphy, *Diplomatic Retreat of France*, 31–32.

11. Schama, *Citizens*, 82.

12. Quoted in Alfred A. Cave, "The Delaware Prophet Neolin: A Reappraisal," *Ethnohistory* 46 (1999): 273.

13. Reuben Gold Thwaites and Louise P. Kellogg, eds., *Documentary History of Dunmore's War, 1774* (Madison: Wisconsin Historical Society, 1905), 378.

14. Anthony F.C. Wallace, *Death and Rebirth of the Seneca* (New York: Random House, 1972), 125; *Jefferson and the Indians: The Tragic Fate of the First Americans* (Cambridge, MA: Harvard University Press, 1999), 78.

15. Wallace, *The Death and Rebirth of the Seneca*, 157.

BIOGRAPHIES:
PEOPLE WHO MADE A DIFFERENCE IN THE FRENCH AND INDIAN WAR

James Abercromby (1706–81)

The men who served under James Abercromby, Great Britain's supreme commander in North America through most of 1758, nicknamed him "Granny." It was not a term of affection. Despite ample military experience, including valiant action in the Netherlands during the War of the Austrian Succession, Abercromby, a Scotsman by birth, was sadly lacking in the qualities that make a successful commanding general. Prior to his appointment as successor to John Campbell, Lord Loudoun, Abercromby had served as a member of Loudoun's staff. The outgoing commander described the Scotsman as a good subordinate, but doubted his suitability for command. Events would soon reveal that Loudoun's appraisal was correct. During Abercromby's watch, British forces in North America mounted three major campaigns against the French. Two were successful: General Jeffrey Amherst took the great French fortress of Louisbourg on Cape Breton Island, and General John Forbes seized the forks of the Ohio as the retreating French forces destroyed Fort Duquesne. The third action, aimed at dislodging the French from Fort Carillon (Ticonderoga) at the southern end of Lake Champlain, should have been the easiest. But it ended in disaster, as a result of Abercromby's bungling.

Abercromby's predecessor, Lord Loudoun, although unpopular with the colonists, was a cool, meticulous officer who believed in careful preparation and in the avoidance of rash action. Abercromby, by contrast, was inconsistent, sometimes rash and sometimes indecisive. He had under his command ample manpower and artillery to drive General Louis Montcalm's relatively weak garrison from Fort Carillon, but he was disturbed by rumors of French reinforcements marching to Lake Champlain and heartened by reports that the defensive works at Fort Carillon had not yet been completed. The first rumor was false; the second, misleading. But both inspired Abercromby to order an immediate attack before his artillery could be emplaced to bombard the French position. Fort Carillon in fact was protected by a maze of fallen timber containing numerous sharpened logs and branches. Its defenses were impenetrable to soldiers attacking on foot.

For four hours Abercromby's troops hurled themselves against that barrier and were shot down by gunfire from the French garrison. Abercromby, receiving reports of the carnage at his headquarters behind the lines, finally decided to break off the action. About 1,500 men, around a tenth of his army, had been wounded or killed in that engagement. Abercromby still possessed a numerical advantage, and had he deployed his artillery, the British could easily have taken the fort. But he decided instead to order a general retreat, leaving Montcalm in control of the southern shore of Lake Champlain. The men under his command, professional soldiers and militia enlistees alike, knew that a sure victory had been thrown away and lives needlessly squandered by an incompetent commander. Abercromby was recalled to England late in the year. His irresponsible performance in America did not, however, block his advancement in rank. Abercromby was promoted to lieutenant general in 1759 and to general in 1772. The remainder of his career was unexceptional and undistinguished.

Jeffrey Amherst, First Lord Amherst (1717–97)

A career soldier, Jeffrey Amherst served as aide-de-camp to both General John Ligonier and the duke of Cumberland during the War of the Austrian Succession. With the outbreak of the Seven Years' War, he was first sent to central Europe to serve with Hessian mercenaries in the pay of Great Britain. In October 1757, Ligonier, now head of the British army, called upon him to lead the expeditionary force sent to capture the French fortress of Louisbourg on Cape Breton Island. It was Amherst's first battlefield command. Arriving off Louisbourg in the spring of 1758, Amherst conducted a protracted, difficult, yet ultimately successful siege. After Abercromby's defeat at Fort Carillon, Amherst was named his successor as commander of British forces in North America. Thorough, meticulous, a bit plodding in his preparations, he took few chances, but pressed forward methodically with long established plans to dislodge the French. He dispatched General John Prideaux to Fort Niagara, at the entrance to Lake Erie. That crucial post fell to the British in July 1759. Amherst himself resumed the attack on Fort Carillon, and in time succeeded where Abercromby had failed. He fell behind schedule and was not able to support General James Wolfe's siege of Quebec, but he resumed the offensive in the summer of 1760. A British army took Montreal and secured the surrender of New France.

Had his career in America ended at that point, Amherst would be remembered as one of the more effective, but less colorful, officers of the French and Indian War. But his mistreatment of the Indians, for whom he had no respect, after the cessation of hostilities helped provoke, if it did not cause, Pontiac's uprising. Stubborn and opinionated, Amherst refused to listen to Indian agents who warned him of the consequences of withholding gifts to longtime Indian allies and of the dangers inherent in his restrictive trade policies. Amherst proved himself highly vindictive during Pontiac's rebellion. He demanded that the leaders of the uprising be hanged, and distributed blankets infected with smallpox in the hope of exterminating much of the Indian population. After his recall in the winter of 1763–64, his successors negotiated a more humane peace than Amherst would have condoned.

Amherst's later career was marked by many honors and little real accomplishment. When the government insisted that he reside in the colony, he resigned the governorship of Virginia. He twice declined to command troops sent to America to suppress the independence movement, not out of respect for the colonists but because of his distaste for the prospect of living once again in America. Even so, his career flourished. He served two long terms as commander in chief of Great Britain's army, and in that capacity suppressed the anti-Catholic Gordon riots in 1780. Before his death he received the title Baron Amherst and promotion to the rank of field marshal.

Edward Braddock (1695–1755)

The defeat and death of General Edward Braddock near the forks of the Ohio in July 1755 has long been regarded as a cardinal example of the perils of using conventional military tactics in an unconventional war. Braddock, son of a career army man, had nearly half a century of experience at the time of his appointment to lead British forces in North America. He was not, however, considered one of Britain's more accomplished officers. Although he had seen action in the Netherlands during the War of the Austrian Succession, Braddock had relatively little battlefield experience. He was a military bureaucrat, a reasonably competent administrator accustomed to working behind the lines. Some believe that his appointment reveals that the British government did not place a particularly high priority on ejecting the French from the contested areas in North America.

Upon his arrival in America, Braddock summoned five of the key colonial governors to Alexandria, Virginia, for a conference on strategy. The overall war plan was approved without much difficulty. British forces, primarily composed of local militia, would occupy and fortify the forks of the Ohio. They would strike the French on the borders of Nova Scotia, and at Crown Point and Fort Niagara in New York. But Braddock's plan to establish a war chest to pay for those campaigns hit a snag. The governors informed him that he could not simply requisition money and materiel. He must obtain the consent of the colonial assemblies. As he gathered his army to march into western Pennsylvania, the general was plagued by shortages. The meat furnished by contractors was often rotten. Prices were extortionate; wagons, in short supply. As for the Indian auxiliaries everyone warned him he must have, he found it difficult to relate to "savages" and antagonized the powerful Delaware chief Shingas by remarking that Indians, being uncivilized, ought not to inherit the land. Intertribal bickering and colonial rivalries also impeded Indian recruitment. Governor Glen of South Carolina sabotaged plans to raise a force of Catawbas and Cherokees to serve with Braddock. When his army entered western Pennsylvania, only eight Indians, remnants of a larger group of Iroquois recruited by the Indian trader George Croghan, remained with him.

In explaining the disaster that ensued, Braddock's few defenders over the years have pointed to the lack of support from the colonists as the prime reason for his failure. More often, however, historians emphasize his negligence in not sending out scouts and his insistence, after blundering into an ambush, that his men form a skirmish line in a wooded area overrun by snipers. It is telling that after the battle, two men independently claimed that they had shot the general because he would not allow them to retreat and find cover. Their story could not be confirmed. No one has questioned Braddock's courage; four horses were shot from under him before someone fired the bullet that, after four days of agony, killed the general. But his battlefield judgment was poor. He was not the right person for that command.

Louis Antoine, Count of Bougainville (1729–1811)

Of all the officers who fought in the French and Indian War, few had as colorful a career as Louis Antoine, count of Bougainville. Senior aide-de-camp to Louis Joseph, marquis of Montcalm, Bougainville, unlike his superior officer, had not been trained as a soldier. Educated at the University of Paris, he was a lawyer by profession and a very gifted and much-published mathematician by avocation. His accomplishments in mathematics won him election to the Royal Society during a brief stint in London on the staff of the French embassy in 1754. Later in life, he made important contributions to ethnology as well.

Bougainville obtained his military commission in 1753, at the age of twenty-four. Attached to Montcalm's expeditionary force, he first saw action in New York during the attack on Fort Oswego in 1756. He later participated in the assault on Fort William Henry (1757) and the defense of Fort Carillon (1758). He won Montcalm's regard as a brave officer of great intelligence. In January 1759, Bougainville arrived back in France on a mission to plead Montcalm's case for unequivocal military authority (the marquis was embroiled in a power struggle with Governor Pierre Vaudreuil) and for substantial reinforcements. He was successful in winning the government's support for the first of these requests; Montcalm's status as supreme commander was confirmed. But on the matter of New France's need for a major infusion of manpower, he failed. The King's ministers were preoccupied with the war in central Europe, and ordered Montcalm to make do with minimal new resources until victory was won in Europe.

Shortly after Bougainville's return from Paris in the spring of 1759, General James Wolfe's army besieged Quebec. In the crucial final battle for the city several months later, Montcalm failed to coordinate his operations with Bougainville, who commanded 1,200 men on the riverfront. Montcalm struck Wolfe's army on the Plains of Abraham before Bougainville could come to his aid. Montcalm's critics then and ever since have argued that he thereby forfeited the battle. After Montcalm's death and Quebec's surrender, Bougainville assisted in the ill-fated defense of Montreal.

Following the surrender of Canada in 1760, Bougainville returned to France. He fought for a time in central Europe, then received a naval commission. He saw action in several theaters of combat, including North America, where the French navy came to the aid of the American revolutionaries. The most notable aspect of his naval service, however, was not military. His meticulous and sympathetic observations of Tahitian culture, published after a Pacific voyage of discovery, made a significant contribution to the fledgling science of ethnology. Bougainville's scientific accomplishments were recognized in his election to the French Academy of Sciences in 1789.

After retiring from the navy in 1792, Bougainville taught for a time, then was imprisoned briefly during the Reign of Terror. Rehabilitated by the Directory (the government that succeeded the Jacobins and ruled from 1795 to 1799), he later enjoyed the favor of Napoleon, who made him a senator and awarded him a title. Bougainville died at the age of eighty-one and was buried among France's elite in the Pantheon.

John Campbell, Fourth Earl of Loudoun (1705–82)

Historians generally agree that the appointment in 1756 of John Campbell, earl of Loudoun, as Governor William Shirley's replacement as British military commander in North America was unfortunate. Imperious and tactless, Loudoun soon antagonized colonial militia officers, whose independence he resented; colonial assemblies, whose prerogatives he did not care to recognize; and, on occasion, royal governors, who had to cope with the problems he created. Armed with orders giving him sweeping powers as captain general and governor in chief of Virginia, Loudoun issued peremptory directives to the colonies demanding money, supplies, and men in the quantities he deemed necessary to carry out the invasion of Canada. He encountered much passive resistance and some open opposition. Enlistments lagged, financial support was not forthcoming, and colonies balked at providing housing for British soldiers. In Philadelphia, some of those soldiers died of exposure as the city delayed the construction of appropriate barracks. In some towns, Loudoun's recruiters were attacked by mobs. He failed to win popular support for his war measures. He did not understand the need to do so.

It is not surprising that his forces accomplished little on the battlefield, although in fairness it must be conceded that Loudoun was not personally responsible for everything that went wrong during his command.

But the overall record was damning. British efforts to drive the French from Lake Champlain failed. Plans to take Louisbourg came to nothing. A French offensive succeeded in taking both Fort Oswego and Fort William Henry, thereby endangering British control of New York.

Loudoun's appointment to the supreme command in North America owed much to the patronage of the duke of Cumberland, favored son of King George II. Cumberland was discredited by his mismanagement of the defense of Hanover in 1757. The rise to power of the "Great Commoner," William Pitt, who had no use for Cumberland, undermined Loudoun's position. Pitt had no reason not to hold Loudoun strictly accountable for his failures, and relieved him of command at the end of 1757.

Despite his dismal record on the battlefield, John Campbell was an able soldier who did make a contribution to the ultimate British victory in North America. His haughty demeanor and lavish lifestyle offended the colonials, and on the surface the earl seemed to have little, if any, regard for anything American. But he was in fact an avid student of frontier warfare. He initiated training programs that combined traditional British army discipline with new techniques of warfare suited to the wilderness. He deemphasized the European-style standing battle line, encouraging troops to fire from a prone position, and in combat to hide behind trees and other natural barriers. Loudoun also stressed the importance of proper use of flanking parties. He had listened to the stories of earlier British defeats, and learned from them. He took counsel from unconventional fighters such as Robert Rogers. Though a thoughtful and careful commander and administrator, Loudoun was a very poor politician, and his lack of skill in dealing with those who might have advanced the war effort proved fatal to his hopes. After his recall, Loudoun remained in the army, but was never given another major command. It was left for others in England and America to learn from his mistakes and profit from his accomplishments.

Etienne-François, Duke of Choiseul (1719–85)

Choiseul, a prominent member of the French government during the reign of Louis XV, was one of the few truly able ministers to enjoy the patronage of the king's powerful mistress, Madame de Pompadour. Through her intervention, he was granted a dukedom in 1758. A year later he was in control of the French war effort. Although he had earlier played a key role in the negotiation of the ill-conceived alliance with Austria, Choiseul now sought to reverse the previous policy of neglecting the overseas conflict with Great Britain in order to pour resources into the campaigns in Europe. In August 1761 he successfully negotiated an alliance with Spain, an accomplishment that led key members of the British government to consider the advisability of making peace. British naval supremacy frustrated his efforts to reverse the course of the world war, but the political upheaval in Great Britain that forced the retirement of Pitt gave Choiseul the opportunity to negotiate a compromise peace settlement. The peace treaty confirmed France's loss of Canada and of her holdings in India, transferred Louisiana to Spain, and restored British control of Minorca. But Choiseul succeeded in protecting the French sugar colonies in the Caribbean, and for that reason claimed a diplomatic victory. The settlement was popular in a war-weary nation humiliated by military defeats.

An opponent of Jesuit influence in the French government early in his career, Choiseul was a champion of modernization. He reformed the army and the navy, supported the expansion of commerce and industry, and promoted overseas trade. A shrewd courtier, wise in the ways of the world, he masterminded an espionage network so extensive that Empress Catherine the Great of Russia complained that his agents infested every court. The most able member of Louis XV's generally incompetent government, Choiseul was disliked by the king's new favorite, Madame Du Barry, and fell from favor. Although still in his prime, Choiseul retired from government permanently in 1770. His removal epitomized the triumph of favoritism over competence in France's Old Regime.

Louis Joseph, Marquis of Montcalm (1712–59)

Born at his family's seat, the chateau of Candiac near Nîmes in the south of France, Montcalm, celebrated after his death as the valiant but doomed defender of Quebec, was the heir of a noble but land-poor provincial family. An able, indeed brilliant, student educated by a tutor, Montcalm as a young child attained a remarkable proficiency in both Latin and Greek. His love of learning and of the classics, unusual for a career soldier, would last all of his life. But for a member of the nobility, heir to a title, the life of a humble scholar was not deemed appropriate. Nor could he enjoy the leisure of a wealthy landowner. Hence, at age fifteen, Montcalm enlisted in the army. Two years later, his father bought him a commission. After his father's death in 1735, Montcalm enhanced his rather shaky financial position by marrying the socially prominent

Angelique Louise Talon de Boulay. A devoted husband and father, Montcalm sired ten children.

His military career flourished. In 1734, he fought in the War of the Polish Succession. In the War of the Austrian Succession, Montcalm commanded a regiment. In 1746, in the battle against the Austrians at Piacenza, Italy (a battle the French lost), Montcalm was severely wounded and taken prisoner. After his return to France, he was promoted to brigadier general and sent back into battle, where he sustained further wounds before the war ended in 1748.

Montcalm's appointment in 1756 to the command of French forces in Canada brought to the war in America a battle-tested and battle-scarred veteran notable for both his intelligence and his courage. But Montcalm's actual record in North America falls far short of romantic images of the great commander and martyr. Montcalm was ill suited for a frontier command. He neither understood nor respected his Native American allies, but regarded them as brutal and cowardly savages. In his early battles in New York, Montcalm could not control his Indian auxiliaries, who massacred some of his British and colonial prisoners of war. In his later engagements, he was unable to obtain much Indian support. Cautious and thoughtful by nature, Montcalm clashed repeatedly with the governor of New France, the Canadian-born Pierre François Rigard, marquis of Vaudreuil. He often defied the governor's orders—refusing, for example, to mount an aggressive offensive in New York after his victory at Fort William Henry in 1757. Montcalm did not respect the Canadian militia, trusting only regular troops from France. His relationships with the *habitants* (settlers) and with officials in New France were often marred by his aloof, almost disdainful manner. After his death, some of his critics claimed that his inability to work effectively with other officers contributed to his defeat by General James Wolfe on the Plains of Abraham and to the loss of Quebec in 1759.

Despite the romantic image of Montcalm once fashionable in the United States, his reputation in Canada has been mixed. Some Canadian historians have faulted him for his failure to use the Canadian militia and its Indian auxiliaries to advantage, and for an excessive caution bordering on defeatism. Some argue that his failure to exploit British weaknesses in 1756 led directly to the loss of Canada, for he did not press the war at a time when it might have been won. A scholar, a gentleman, an aristocrat, and a good soldier steeped in European traditions of war, Montcalm was ill suited to the needs of an unconventional and brutal wilderness war.

William Pitt, First Earl of Chatham (1708–78)

The appointment of William Pitt ("the Great Commoner") as secretary of state in December 1756 led to the transformation of the British war effort. Born into a middle-class family of means, Pitt studied at Trinity College, Oxford, but ill health forced him to withdraw before completing his degree. Throughout his life, Pitt suffered from gout. After convalescing in Europe, he returned to England and through the good offices of his sister-in-law obtained an appointment as an officer in a crack cavalry unit, the King's Own Regiment of Horse. At the age of twenty-seven, he succeeded his brother as representative in Parliament for Old Sarum. Pitt soon emerged as a major spokesman for the opposition faction, known as the Patriot Whigs, whose platform called for a more aggressive, anti-Spanish policy in defense of imperial interests. No friends to the German-born king, George II, or to his prime minister, Robert Walpole, the Patriot Whigs opposed the heavy subsidies devoted to the defense of Hanover. Pitt and other members of his faction who sympathized with the king's estranged first son, Frederick Louis, prince of Wales, proposed a resolution on the occasion of the prince's marriage which the king found very offensive. George II retaliated by securing the revocation of Pitt's army commission. Not surprisingly, soon after Pitt became secretary of state, the king took advantage of a dispute between Pitt and a coalition partner, George Grenville, to force Pitt out of office in April 1757. Popular clamor in his support, however, led to his recall several months later. Samuel Johnson later quipped, "Walpole was a minister given by the Crown to the people; Pitt was a minister given by the people to the Crown."[1]

Pitt transformed Great Britain's military priorities. Rather than centering offensive actions in Europe (where King George II was also ruler of the German state of Hanover), he struck hard at France's worldwide colonial empire, utilizing British naval superiority to maximum advantage. The expulsion of France from North America was one of Pitt's highest priorities. Under his leadership, for the first time substantial numbers of regular British army troops were sent to America and committed to the attack on Canada. By removing Lord Loudoun as supreme commander, Pitt repaired damaged relationships with colonial militia units through revoking earlier orders that placed senior militia officers under the command of junior British army officers. He won support from local elites by acknowledging the prerogatives of the elected colonial assemblies. The result of those changes in policy was an upsurge in colonial support for the war effort. Soon a series of victories paved the way for British occupation of Canada. An astute politician, Pitt won the support of the king not only by presenting him with impressive overseas victories, but also by dropping his earlier opposition to British support of the defense of Hanover.

Pitt's achievements in North America were matched throughout the world, as France suffered crushing losses on the high seas, in the Caribbean, in Africa, and in India. In 1761, however, Pitt was forced to resign. Doubts about his uncompromising war policy came to a head when the cabinet refused to follow his lead and widen the offensive by declaring war on Spain. The prudent worried about the cost of a protracted conflict. His political enemies exploited those anxieties to secure a change in leadership. Although George II had come to appreciate Pitt's talents, the new king, George III, favored peace. A new government that took office in 1762 negotiated a peace settlement with France that enhanced Great Britain's power and extended her possessions, but fell short of Pitt's greatest aspirations. He complained bitterly that the Treaty of Paris (1763) was far too lenient.

Pitt's parliamentary faction regained control of the government in 1766, but although ostensibly their leader, Pitt, whose health was always problematic, was now too ill to play a major role. He stepped down as prime minister in 1768, but remained a man of great influence. As a member of Parliament, he opposed the Stamp Act and other legislation intended to tax the colonies, denying that the British government had the right to levy such taxes without the colonists' consent. He also spoke out against the coercive measures that provoked the American Revolution, but opposed the granting of American independence. He died before the North American colonies were lost.

An imposing man with a magnificent speaking voice and a sure command of language, Pitt was one of the great orators of his age. He was arguably the greatest British politician and statesman of the eighteenth century.

Pontiac (1720?–69)

In 1746, a young Ottawa warrior from a village on an island in the Maumee River of northwest Ohio joined a band of warriors determined

to fight for the French in King George's War. Nothing is known of his earlier history, but during the years of uneasy peace after the war, Pontiac
settled in a village near the French outpost at Detroit. When war broke
out anew in 1754, he once again fought against the British. He may have
been among the warriors who ambushed and defeated Braddock. The
evidence confirms that he participated in other frontier raids, although his
name was not yet known to his British adversaries.

Pontiac was a deeply religious man, head of a secret, sacred society
known as the Metai. No admirer of either Christianity or European culture, he was inspired, in the immediate years after France's defeat, by the
teachings of a Delaware visionary whom he called, after his clan, the Wolf.
We now know him as Neolin, a prophet who taught that the survival of
Indians would be possible only through the rejection of Europeans and
all their works. Claiming that he had visited heaven and consulted the
Creator, whom he called "the Master of Life," Neolin conveyed God's demand that Indians abandon their tribal feuds, eschew witchcraft and con-
juring, prohibit the use of alcohol, and free themselves of all the trappings
of European culture: clothing, domesticated animals, ultimately even guns
and metal implements. If this were done, the Master of Life would em-
power Indians and enable them to drive the whites out of the land. If it
were not done, however, they were doomed to misery and sickness in this
world, and would suffer the eternal pain of hellfire in the next. Inspired
by Neolin's vision, Pontiac memorized the story of his vision and repeated
it to his warriors to give them courage and hope. But as a practical man
who understood the realities of frontier warfare, he modified Neolin's an-
tiwhite message to permit continued dealings with the French.

The heavy-handed actions of Jeffrey Amherst, the British commander
in North America, after the war provoked widespread panic and anger
among the Indian nations of the interior. Amherst refused to continue the
practice of gift giving, not caring that he was thereby committing an act
tantamount to a declaration of war, for in Indian cultures gift giving symbolized the renewal of fictive kinship. He also raised the price of goods
Indians needed to buy and restricted their availability, as well as seizing
some Iroquois land to give to certain favorites among his officers. Warned
that his actions could provoke an Indian war, he scoffed at the notion that
"savages" could do any real damage.

Amherst was mistaken. Indian uprisings broke out in several frontier areas in 1763, and they did great damage. In the north, Pontiac, head

of a loose confederation, besieged Detroit. Warriors overran seven forts in the upper Great Lakes region, Indiana, Michigan, and western Pennsylvania. But the major forts—Detroit, Pitt, and Niagara—held out. Pontiac, short of food and other supplies, abandoned the siege of Detroit and moved west late in 1763. He made peace with the British in October 1764 and was granted fairly generous terms on the condition that he would persuade others to lay down their arms. Some, including a Shawnee band, refused to do so, and fought on for several months in 1765. Pontiac resettled in the Illinois country, and was killed by an Indian rival in 1769.

Robert Rogers (1732–95)

During the French and Indian war, Major Robert Rogers, commander of Rogers's Rangers, was transformed into a folk hero. A careful scrutiny of his background, war record, and later life suggests that the real Rogers was far more interesting and complex than the mythic frontiersman celebrated in popular fiction and romantic histories.

Rogers grew up in New Hampshire, a rough frontier region that had been the target of French-inspired Indian raids for half a century. He first fought Indians as a fourteen-year-old militia volunteer. A poorly educated, large, and robust man of modest means, the young Rogers tried his hand at farming but also became involved in some very questionable business dealings that led to his trial and acquittal on a charge of counterfeiting. With the outbreak of the French and Indian War, he joined New Hampshire forces committed to the attack on the French fort at Crown Point. Colonel William Johnson, commander of that abortive operation, assigned Rogers the task of conducting a reconnaissance mission to determine the location of the French army and its Indian allies. He found that assignment most congenial, and soon not only was commander of a permanent ranger unit but also was charged with responsibility for training others in the art of irregular wilderness warfare. His men traveled light, moved fast, and struck without warning, taking both prisoners and scalps.

Rogers's actual military record did not quite live up to the myth. Although there is no doubt that he made an important contribution to the war effort, his unit sometimes suffered high losses, and on occasion even got lost in the woods. Moreover, in his raid on the Indian village of St. Francis, he chose to disregard the explicit orders of General Amherst to spare women and children, and massacred about 200 people. He justified his action by claiming that white scalps were hanging from poles in the village. But neither Amherst nor the British public was much concerned with the loss of Indian lives. Rogers was lionized.

The postwar years were difficult for Robert Rogers. He was never paid adequately for either his services or his expenses, and found himself deep in debt. His efforts to make his fortune through the Indian trade and through land speculation all ended badly. Although he fought against both the Cherokees and Pontiac's insurgents, he was unable, after Amherst's recall, to establish a satisfactory relationship with either Amherst's successor, General Thomas Gage, or with Indian Superintendant Sir William Johnson. In 1765 Rogers, hounded by creditors, fled to London, where he published a well-received volume of memoirs and sought patronage. His quest for an appointment succeeded. Rogers returned to America in 1766 as the commandant of the British outpost at Michilimackinac (Mackinac) in the upper Great Lakes region.

As commandant, Rogers soon established a good relationship with the local Indians, but ran afoul of other British officials close to Gage and Johnson. He was arrested and imprisoned on trumped-up charges of treason (presumed collusion with the French) and mismanagement of funds (excessive generosity to Indians). Tried in Montreal in 1768, Rogers was acquitted but not restored to his command. His financial situation grew desperate, and he spent time in debtor's prison as his pleas for recompense for his wartime services went unheeded.

Soon after the outbreak of the American Revolution, Rogers was incarcerated on orders of George Washington, who suspected him of being a British spy. He escaped, and made his way to the British lines. General Thomas Howe, brother of an officer and friend of Rogers killed at the siege of Fort Carillon in 1758, placed him in command of a ranger unit. But Rogers did not fare well in the British army, and he was dismissed within a year. The old frontier fighter resettled in London, where he lived in poverty and obscurity until his death in 1795.

William Shirley (1694–1771)

The frustrations and the failure of Governor William Shirley, Braddock's successor as British commander in chief in North America, reveal much about the weaknesses of the British war effort in the early years of the conflict.

Shirley was an able colonial civil servant, educated at Cambridge and at the Inner Temple. Admitted to the bar in 1720, he spent a number of

years practicing law in London. His involvement in a notorious speculation known as the South Sea Island Bubble of 1720 resulted in the loss of
his wife's estate, and led Shirley to seek new opportunities. Soon after the
collapse of the Bubble, the Shirley family migrated to Boston, where he
served as advocate general of the Vice Admiralty Court and built up a
lucrative law practice. Well connected on both sides of the Atlantic, Shirley
was named royal governor of Massachusetts in 1741.

Governor Shirley was an ardent supporter of the war against France
which broke out in 1744 (King George's War). He masterminded a spec-
tacular and successful assault on the great French fortress of Louisbourg
on Cape Breton Island. He was deeply disappointed when the fortress and
the island were returned to France in the Treaty of Aix-la-Chapelle (1748).
Dispatched to France as part of a delegation charged with negotiating a
settlement of boundary disputes in North America, Shirley was opposed
to concessions and looked to the revival of war with France as an opportunity to acquire northern territories at her expense.

After hostilities erupted on the Pennsylvania frontier, Shirley collabo-
rated with General Braddock in drawing up plans to counter the French
territorial offensive that contemplated military action in western Pennsylvania, northern New York, and Nova Scotia. Drawing on his connections
to secure appointment as Braddock's successor in 1755, Shirley planned
an ambitious offensive against French positions on the New York frontier.
He was undercut at every step of the way by jealous and resentful New
York politicians and other rivals who interfered with his access to men,
supplies, munitions, and Indian allies. His army never reached its objectives. A French counterattack took Fort Oswego in 1756. His enemies
secured Shirley's recall to London, where he faced charges of military incompetence and misuse of funds. He was exonerated, but played no further role in the campaigns against New France. Appointed governor of the
Bahamas, he served with distinction in that post for six years, then returned
to Massachusetts, where he lived in retirement until his death in 1771.

Theyanoguin (Chief Hendrick) (1675?–1755)

The security of the colony of New York depended on the goodwill
of the members of the League of the Iroquois. Throughout the colonial
era, the British and the French vied for Iroquois support. In that contest,
Great Britain had no better friend than Theyanoguin, a Mohawk sachem
they called King Hendrick.

Theyanoguin was born in Massachusetts around the time of King Philip's War; the exact date is unknown. His father was Mohican; his mother, Mohawk. By virtue of the principles of matrilineal descent observed by the Iroquois, Theyanoguin was a Mohawk, a member of the Wolf clan. He quickly rose to prominence, and was one of the signers of the Anglo-Iroquois Treaty of 1701 that granted the English rights in the Ohio country. As a young man, he had joined the Dutch Reformed Church and served occasionally as a preacher. He was not, however, subservient to whites. In 1698, he exposed a land fraud perpetrated by the pastor who had converted him, and secured both the return of Iroquois land and the pastor's dismissal. Despite that incident, he supported the British struggle against French and Catholic influence in Iroquois country. In 1709, Theyanoguin volunteered to raise warriors in support of a proposed raid on Canada. The raid never occurred, but Theyanoguin and three other pro-English Indian leaders traveled to London at crown expense a year later. There they met Queen Anne and were lionized by the public, and returned home laden with gifts.

A member of the great council of the League of the Iroquois, which met at Onondaga, Theyanoguin at first was sympathetic to the efforts of the London-based Society for the Propagation of the Gospel, which hoped to convert the Iroquois to Protestant Christianity, but he later became quite critical of the missionaries and opposed their financial demands. The Mohawk clan matrons for that reason expelled him from the League council in 1713. Remaining close to the British despite his ambivalent feelings about their missionaries, Theyanoguin in 1722 tried, unsuccessfully, to serve as an intermediary to settle the conflict between the Abenaki and the New England colonists. He made a second trip to England in 1740, and was presented to King George II.

During King George's War, Theyanoguin exposed and opposed the efforts of the French to win Mohawk support. He was disappointed, however, by New York's failure to take decisive action to expel the French. He accompanied a Mohawk delegation to Montreal in 1746. Although he met with French officials and received their gifts, Chief Hendrick was not won over. On his way home, his party attacked and killed members of a French construction crew on the northern shore of Lake Champlain. Closely associated with the British agent William Johnson, he encouraged the Mohawk to supply warriors for the defense of Fort Ontario.

After the war, Theyanoguin was part of a delegation to Albany that complained about inadequate support for Britain's friends and for Johnson, who had resigned from the Indian Service on the grounds that he could no longer personally bear the expense. They received little encouragement from New York officials. However, the Board of Trade in London, alarmed by reports of Iroquois disaffection, soon thereafter ordered New York's governor to call a conference of both Iroquois representatives and spokesmen of other colonies to repair the damage. The Albany Congress of 1754 was poorly attended. At its sessions, Theyanoguin was outspoken and eloquent in his condemnation of British commercial abuses, including fraudulent land sales and the trade in alcohol. (He was not, however, opposed to all land transactions, having used his influence in 1751 to secure an enormous tract for William Johnson. Nor did he call for a total ban of alcohol sales.) Theyanoguin's cutting remarks about colonial disunity have led some scholars to argue that the League of the Iroquois was the model for the Constitution of the United States. (They are, however, very dissimilar forms of government.) His arguments and complaints elicited promises of reform from colonial officials.

With the outbreak of the French and Indian War, Theyanoguin recruited warriors to fight for Great Britain and, although old and rather infirm, accompanied his friend William Johnson into the battle at Lake George. He died in combat on September 7, 1755. The clan matrons forbade further Mohawk involvement in the war, a prohibition that was not lifted until it was clear that the French defeat was inevitable.

Pierre François de Rigaud de Vaudreuil (1698-1778)

The Canadian-born son of Philippe de Rigaud de Vaudreuil, governor of New France from 1703 to 1725, began his career as a soldier. He was first commissioned, as an ensign, at the age of ten. In 1721, as a young captain, he participated in a military expedition that explored Lake Ontario and secured from the Seneca and Onondaga members of the Iroquois League permission to construct Fort Niagara at the lake's western entrance. In 1727 Vaudreuil fought against the Fox Indians of the upper Great Lakes. Six years later, he left military service to accept a civil commission as governor of Trois Rivieres. A greater challenge came his way in 1743 when Vaudreuil was named governor of Louisiana. For the next ten years he grappled with the problems of securing his isolated and underpopulated colony. The tiny, ill-equipped French garrison could not do the job. Louisiana of necessity relied on Indian allies. But during the War of the Austrian Succession the British had infiltrated the Choctaw nation, formerly friendly to France. A strong faction of the Choctaws now turned on their former allies. Vaudreuil, although short of supplies with which to buy back Choctaw loyalty, managed through skillful diplomacy to encourage the pro-French faction, which prevailed in the ensuing Choctaw civil war. The Choctaw victors killed some British agents and traders, and drove others from their territory. The greatly feared British assault on New Orleans did not materialize.

After ten years as governor of Louisiana, Vaudreuil resettled in Paris in 1753. He was recalled to North America in 1755, assuming the post of governor of New France. His record in Canada was mixed. Under his administration, the official corruption that earlier had prompted the French government to consider the abandonment of the colony continued unabated. Vaudreuil's major task was to defend Canada against an anticipated British offensive. Corrupt officeholders, led by the intendant Francois Bigot, drained the colony of materiel needed by the militia and the army. Outnumbered and possessing only limited resources, Vaudreuil nonetheless set in motion an audacious plan to attack the British on the frontier wherever they were vulnerable, and thereby keep the enemy off balance. Aggressive action, he believed, could deny the British the opportunity to stage a massive invasion of Canada, and thereby overcome New France's numerical disadvantage.

In carrying out that strategy, Vaudreuil relied heavily on both the Canadian militia and his Indian allies. His direction of the war was undercut by the professional military officers dispatched from France to defend the colony. In particular, the commander of the regular French troops, Louis de Montcalm, was unfamiliar with conditions in North America, and had little understanding of Vaudreuil's plan. Montcalm refused to cooperate with the governor's insistence on waging an offensive war, terminating the invasion of New York after his victory at Fort William Henry in 1757. In the ensuing controversy between the governor and the general, Paris backed Montcalm and ordered Vaudreuil to defer to him. Historians have generally taken Montcalm's side in that dispute, but it can be argued that Vaudreuil had the better understanding of the nature of war in the New World. In fact, both men must share the blame for the loss of Quebec to General James Wolfe in 1759. The invasion route from the sea to Quebec via the St. Lawrence River could have been rendered unusable by proper placement of artillery batteries on shore. Vaudreuil's strategic planning made inadequate provision for defense in that quarter. Moreover, shortly before Wolfe attacked, the governor inexplicably ordered the evacuation of a regiment that Montcalm had placed on the Plains of Abraham. Montcalm, it is generally agreed, made a fatal error when he engaged Wolfe's forces before all of his reinforcements were in place. He attacked a stronger force on the Plains of Abraham, and lost both the battle and his life. There is thus ample reason to fault both the governor and the general.

The failure of France to reinforce Canada after the fall of Quebec doomed Vaudreuil's efforts to regain the initiative. Although no longer plagued by dissension within the army, he now simply lacked the means to resist General Jeffrey Amherst's invasion force. In 1760, he surrendered at Montreal. The terms Amherst dictated were severe and humiliating, but Vaudreuil knew that further resistance would only lead to a bloodbath in which most of his troops and many civilians would perish. He therefore disregarded Paris's demand that he fight to the death rather than accept dishonor, and signed the capitulation. Canada was now in the hands of the British army.

Upon his return to France in 1760, Vaudreuil was arrested and placed on trial for his conduct in the loss of Canada. He was acquitted by the court, but has not fared as well with posterity. The former governor spent the rest of his life in retirement in Paris.

George Washington (1732–99)

George Washington, "the father of his country," is remembered primarily as the leader of the American army that won independence and as the first president of the United States. But as a young man Washington played an important role in the French and Indian War. His experiences in that conflict profoundly influenced his feelings about the mother country.

Born into a landed, slaveholding Virginia family that had experienced some loss of means, Washington was orphaned during his boyhood. He was raised at Mount Vernon, the plantation inherited by his half brother

Lawrence. As a young man, Washington learned the surveyor's trade but longed for a military career, eagerly reading books on the art of war. In 1752, when George was nineteen, his half brother died, and he inherited Mount Vernon. Washington's marriage seven years later to a propertied widow, Martha Custis, made him one of the wealthiest men in Virginia.

Before his marriage, the dispute with the France over control of the Old Northwest gave Washington, then twenty-two years old, an opportunity to make his mark as a soldier. But he failed this first test. In the spring of 1754, Washington was placed in command of a militia unit when its commanding officer died unexpectedly. Their orders were to occupy the forks of the Ohio. En route, Washington arrested a detachment of French soldiers but lost control of his Indian escorts, who proceeded to murder several of his prisoners, including the ranking French officer, Ensign Joseph Coulon de Jumonville. Soon thereafter, Washington and his men were besieged in their makeshift Fort Necessity by a superior French force. Upon his surrender, Washington was forced to sign a document confessing to the "murder" of Jumonville. He returned to Virginia not in triumph but on parole.

The following year (1755) Washington served as a civilian aid to General Edmund Braddock. It was a disillusioning experience. The British general was arrogant and inept. After Braddock's death in an ambush near the forks of the Ohio, the British army he had led beat a hasty and, in Washington's view, unnecessary retreat. The whole affair struck the young Virginian as disgraceful and dishonorable. Washington's subsequent military service, as commander of the Virginia militia guarding the frontier, was also a very unhappy experience. The British commanders with whom he dealt cared little about the safety of the western settlers. Washington lacked even minimal resources, and on occasion his men were taken from him and assigned to protect coastal plantations endangered by potential slave revolts.

An ambitious man, Washington at one time hoped to receive a commission in the regular British army. But it was soon apparent that, given the attitude of British officers toward the "colonials," he had no real future in Great Britain's service. Washington was one of a number of wealthy members of the colonial elite stung by the condescension of a British establishment that regarded them as rustic inferiors. Other, larger issues, such as concern for the protection of Virginians' claim to enjoy "the rights of

Englishmen," explain the ultimate transformation of George Washington into a revolutionary. But some of the sources of his disillusionment with British rule are to be traced to his years as a Virginia militia officer in the French and Indian War.

James Wolfe (1727–59)

The conqueror of Quebec was born in Kent, the son of a career soldier who attained the rank of lieutenant general. At the age of fourteen, Wolfe was commissioned a second lieutenant in his father's regiment. Transferred to another infantry unit, he saw action in Flanders during the War of the Austrian Succession. Promoted while still in his teens to the rank of brigade major, Wolfe in 1745 participated in the duke of Cumberland's brutal campaign in Scotland against the Stuart pretender to the British throne. He was present at the bloody final battle at Culloden Moor, which claimed the lives of a third of his regiment. The following year he fought in the Netherlands, was wounded, returned to England for a brief convalescence, then returned to military duty in the Low Countries. Considered a model officer, Wolfe at the age of twenty-two was promoted to lieutenant colonel and given command of a regiment.

After a brief leave of absence devoted to study in Dublin and Paris in 1752, Wolfe returned to his command, rapidly earning a reputation as a strict and exacting disciplinarian. At the beginning of the Seven Years' War in 1757, his regiment took part in an unsuccessful raid on the French coast. A greater opportunity came Wolfe's way in the following year, when he was given command of a brigade attached to the expeditionary force, commanded by Lord Jeffrey Amherst, that was committed to the capture of Louisbourg at the entrance to the St. Lawrence River. In that engagement, Wolfe led a landing party that overran a French shore battery and helped open the way to the successful siege of the fortress. After the fall of Louisbourg, Wolfe was ordered to destroy three small fishing villages on the St. Lawrence. After completing that mission, he sailed for England.

A man of great ambition, often resented by subordinate officers of higher social class, Wolfe used his connections in London to lobby for an independent command. In his efforts to impress potential patrons, he was much inclined to exaggerate his role in the capture of Louisbourg and to deprecate the accomplishments of his commander, General Amherst, whom he portrayed as slow and indecisive. Wolfe hoped to be given a cavalry command with British forces in Europe. Instead, he was tendered command of an expeditionary force under orders to invade Canada by way of the St. Lawrence River and capture Quebec. He seized that opportunity, but after landing near the city found it virtually impregnable. Facing the prospect of abandoning the campaign, Wolfe, having learned about a narrow footpath near Anse au Foulon that ran from the riverfront to the Plains of Abraham on the cliffs above, devised an audacious plan to scale those cliffs, occupy the Plains, and lay siege to the city. Wolfe withheld information about his plan until the last minute. His subordinates were skeptical, but obeyed their orders. Since the governor had previously withdrawn forces that Montcalm had stationed on the Plains of Abraham, the area was lightly defended. The British were even able to drag up some light artillery. The opposing general, Louis de Montcalm, apprised of their presence, made a serious miscalculation. Believing the British force to be weak, he left his encampment and attacked them on the Plains of Abraham. In the battle that ensued, Montcalm's forces were routed; he sustained a fatal wound. Quebec surrendered to the British on September 18, 1759, but General Wolfe did not live to enjoy his triumph. Struck by sniper bullets, he had died several days earlier. He was thirty-two years old.

Although Wolfe was transformed into a popular hero soon after his death, and celebrated in the history books throughout the next two centuries, some military historians who have studied his Quebec campaign in detail have expressed serious doubts about the wisdom of some of his actions. His relationship with his officers was poor, and he did not make the best possible use of their talents. Despite the audacity, and success, of his attack on Quebec, once his forces had reached the Plains of Abraham, he did not devise, let alone put into effect, a well-thought-out battle plan for taking the city. By occupying open ground in front of the city walls, Wolfe placed his troops in great jeopardy. His advance on the city would have ended in disaster had Montcalm not mounted a premature attack. It was Wolfe's good luck that his adversary miscalculated and did not wait for the reinforcements that would have given him the forces needed to repel the invader. In poor health throughout his career, a man of eccentric behavior and morbid temperament, neither liked nor respected by his colleagues, Wolfe nevertheless was awarded posthumous glorification, a striking example of the shifting fortunes of war.

Note

1. Quoted in Noel St. John Williams, *Redcoats Along the Hudson* (London: Brassy's, 1998), 3.

PRIMARY DOCUMENTS OF THE FRENCH AND INDIAN WAR

Document 1
The Governor of New France Warns Indians of British Designs on Their Land, 1749

During his tour of the Ohio country in 1749, Pierre-Joseph Céleron de Blainville, the commandant of the French outpost at Detroit, visited numerous Indian villages to warn them not to trade with the British or allow them to enter their territories. At each village, he read a letter from the marquis of la Galassonière, governor of New France. The first excerpt below is from the letter Céleron read to the inhabitants of a Seneca village the French called La Paille Coupée in northwestern Pennsylvania; the second, from the letter read at a trading village in western Pennsylvania near the strategically crucial forks of the Ohio. Called Logstown by the British, this village had a mixed population of Delawares, Shawnees, and Mingos. Both French and British traders did business there. The flags of both countries flew over the village's rude enclosure. After reading each letter, Céleron told the villagers that they must trade only with the French. He defined the relationship between the French king and the Indians of the Ohio country as that of a father to his children. In most of the villages, he received a polite but cool reception. At Logstown, some of the inhabitants were openly hostile. Although Céleron planted metal plates throughout the Ohio country proclaiming French sovereignty, his mission accomplished little.

My children, since I was at war with the English [a reference to King George's War, recently concluded] I have learned that they have seduced you; and not content with corrupting your hearts, have taken advantage of my absence to invade lands which are not theirs, but mine, and therefore I have resolved to send you Monsieur Céleron, to tell you my intentions, which are that I will not endure the English on my lands. Listen to me, children, mark well the words that I send you, follow my advice, and the sky will always be calm and clear over your village.

Through the love I bear you, my children, I send you Monsieur de Celeron to open your eyes to the designs of the English against your lands. The establishments they mean to make, and of which you are certainly ignorant, tend to complete your ruin. They hide from you their plans, which are to settle here, and drive you away, if I let them. As a good father who tenderly loves his children, and though far away always bears them in his heart, I must warn you of the danger that threatens you. The English intend to rob you of your country, and that they may succeed, they begin by corrupting your minds. As they mean to seize the Ohio, which belongs to me, I send to warn them to retire.

Source: Francis Parkman, *Montcalm and Wolf,* 2 vols. (Boston: Little, Brown, 1884), 2:44, 47.

Document 2
George Croghan's Account of a Diplomatic Confrontation at Logstown, 1751

The British undertook a diplomatic offensive to counter French influence with the Ohio Indians. In May 1751, the veteran Indian trader George Croghan arrived at Logstown, bearing messages from James Hamilton, deputy governor of Pennsylvania, to the Indian nations represented there. Also present at Logstown was Philippe Thomas Joncaire, a highly skilled French forest diplomat whose father had long lived among the Senecas and had gained great influence with that Iroquois nation. The younger Joncaire was instrumental in persuading the Indians of western Pennsylvania and Ohio to support the French in the coming war with Great Britain. George Croghan summarized in his journal speeches which he and Joncaire made to a gathering of Indians at Logstown, and included responses of some of the Indian representatives. In the excerpt given below, Joncaire speaks first, an Iroquois replies, then Croghan addresses the ranking chief from the League of the Iroquois, who responds. As events would later demonstrate, Croghan's journal entries greatly overstate his success at Logstown. His reliance on the Iroquois to deliver the western Indians into the British camp proved to be a serious mistake. Joncaire won support from a number of western tribes who feared the land-hungry British and resented the Iroquois.

May the 21st, 1751—Mr. Ioncoeur [Joncaire] the French interpreter, called a council with all the Indians then present in the town, and made the following speech. "CHILDREN: I desire you may now give me an answer from your hearts to the speech Monsieur Céleron made to you. His speech was, That their Father the Governor of Canada desired his children on the Ohio to turn away the English traders from amongst them, and discharge them from ever coming to trade there again, or any of the branches, on pain of incurring his displeasure. . . ."

Immediately one of the Chiefs of the Six Nations got up and made the following answer. "FATHERS: I mean those who call themselves our Fathers, hear what I am going to say to you. You desire that we may turn our Brothers the English away, and not suffer them to come and trade with us again; I tell you now from our hearts we will not, for we ourselves brought them here to trade with us, and they shall live amongst us as long as there is one of us alive. You are always threatening our Brothers what you will do to them, and particularly to that man (pointing to me); now if you have anything to say to our Brothers tell it to him if you be a man, as you Frenchmen say you are, and the head of all nations. Our Brothers [the British] are the people we will trade with, and not you. . . ."

May 24th, 1751—[Croghan reads a statement to the Iroquois on behalf of Governor Hamilton of Pennsylvania.] I am informed by George Croghan that the French obstruct my traders and carry away their persons and goods, and are guilty of many outrageous practices, whereby the roads are rendered unsafe to travel in, nor can we ask our traders to go amongst you whilst their lives and effects are in such great danger. How comes this to pass? Don't [*sic*] this proceed from the pride of Onontio [the French governor of Canada] whom the Indians call Father because they don't see his ill designs? The strong houses [forts] you give him leave to erect on your lands serve (as your Brethren the English always told you) to impoverish you and keep your wives and children always naked by keeping the English traders at a distance, the French well knowing that the English sell their goods cheaper than they can afford, and I can assure you Onontio will never rest while an English trader comes to Ohio, and indeed if you don't open your eyes and put a stop to his proceedings he will gain his ends. Brethren: I hope you will consider what Onontio means or is about to do.

The Speaker of the Six Nations made the following Speech to Monsieur Ioncoeur [Joncaire] in open council; he spoke very quickly and sharp with the air of a warrior.

"FATHER—how comes it that you have broke the general peace? Is it not three years since you as well as our Brother the English told us there was a peace between the English and the French, and how comes it that you have taken our Brothers [the English] as your prisoners on our lands? I desire that you may go home directly off our lands and tell Onontio to send us word immediately what was his reason for using our brothers so, or what he means by such proceedings, that we may know what to do, for I can assure Onontio that the Six Nations will not take such usage. . . ."

Source: Reuben Gold Thwaites, ed., *Early Western Travels 1748–1846*, 32 vols. (Cleveland: Arthur H. Clark, 1904), 1:59–60, 67–69. In the excerpt printed above, and in the other documents quoted below, both spelling and capitalization have been modernized.

Document 3
Instructions to Governor Duquesne, 1752

In April 1752, the French government approved a memorandum containing the instructions to be given to the marquis de la Duquesne, newly appointed governor of Canada. The excerpt printed below contains a complaint about Duquesne's predecessor, whose handling of Indian relations struck them as rash; a statement of the basis of France's claim to the Ohio valley; and an outline of the reasons why that claim must be maintained. It also provides specific instructions for dealing with both the British and the Indians. Of particular interest in this document is the evidence it provides of Paris's concern for good relations with all the Indian tribes. French policy makers were well aware that their North American holdings could be protected only with the help of Native Americans.

The marquis de la Jonquière [outgoing governor of Canada] has rendered an account of a plan he had prepared both to drive the English from the river and to chastise the Indians who allowed themselves to be gained over. That plan was to dispatch several detachments of Frenchmen and Indian allies. . . . But all the consequent operations reduce themselves to a seizure of some English traders with their goods, and to the murder of two Indians of the Miami nation.

The seizure of the English traders, whose effects have been confiscated and even plundered by our Indians, cannot but produce a good effect, by. . . [intimidating] the other traders of that nation. But the murder of the two Miamis may be attended by unfortunate consequences; and in fact intelligence has been received that it had already caused a great deal of excitement among the rebel Nations [Indians hostile to the French].

The marquis de la Jonquière pretends that if his expedition has not had the success he expected, it was because Sieur Céleron, Major and Commandant of Detroit, which was to be the centre of all the operations, has badly executed the orders and instructions he had given him.

But it would be useless, now, to enter into an examination of the faults that may have been committed. We must start from the present position, and establish some principles upon which his Majesty may issue such orders as he may deem proper.

The English may pretend that we are bound by the Treaty of Utrecht to permit the Indians to trade with them. But it is certain that nothing can oblige us to suffer this trade on our territory. . . . The River Ohio, otherwise called the Beautiful River, and its tributaries belong indisputably to France, by virtue of discovery by Sieur de la Salle; of the trading posts the French have had there since, and of possession which is so much the more unquestionable as it constitutes the most frequent communication from Canada to Louisiana. It is only within a few years that the English have undertaken to trade there; and now they pretend to exclude us from it.

They have not, up to the present time, however, maintained that these rivers belong to them; they pretend only that the Iroquois are masters of them and being the Sovereigns of these Indians, they can exercise their rights. But 'tis certain that these Indians have none, and that, besides, the pretended sovereignty of the English over them is a chimera.

Meanwhile 'tis of the greatest importance to arrest the progress of the pretensions and expeditions of the English in that quarter. Should they succeed there, they would cut off the communications between the two Colonies of Canada and Louisiana, and would be in a position to trouble them, and ruin both one and the other, independent of the advantages they would at once experience in their trade to the prejudice of ours. . . .

It is not known what steps the marquis de la Jonquiere will take this year; but whatever they be, it appears that the orders to be given on this subject to Mr. Duquesne, who is to succeed him in the government, must have principally for their object, to avoid, as much as possible, an Indian war on that account.

Wars of this character are always extremely expensive, and very rarely productive of any real advantage.

Therefore, without undertaking, as the marquis de la Jonquière appears to have proposed, to drive from the River Ohio the Indians who are looked upon as rebels or suspected, and without wishing to destroy the liberty of their trade, it is thought best to adhere to two principal points.

1st. To make every possible effort to drive the English from our territory, and to prevent them coming there to trade.

2nd. To give the Indians to understand at the same time that no harm is intended them, that they will have liberty to go to the English to trade, but will not be allowed to receive them on our territory.

There is good reason to believe that by this course of conduct, by providing our posts with plenty of goods and preventing our traders dictating to the Indians, our trade will recover the superiority over that of the English in these parts; for 'tis certain the Indians do not like to go into their towns, nor forts . . . 'tis considered proper to direct Mr. Duquesne to lay down henceforth a different system from that always followed hitherto in regard to wars among the Indians. With a view to occupy and weaken them, the principle has been to excite and foment these kinds of wars. That was of advantage in the infancy of the settlement of Canada. But in the condition to which these Nations are now reduced . . . it is in every respect more useful that the French perform between them the part of protectors and pacifiers. They will, thereby, entertain more consideration and attachment for us. . . .

Source: E.B. O'Callaghan and B. Fernow, eds., *Documents Relative to the Colonial History of the State of New York*, 15 vols. (Albany, NY: Weed and Parsons, 1853–87), 10:242–44.

Document 4
Theyanoguin Explains Iroquois Grievances
at the Albany Conference, 1754

In 1753, the government of Great Britain received reports from New York indicating that members of the League of the Iroquois were on the verge of throwing their support to the French. The Iroquois not only felt slighted by lack of attention from the province's royal government, but also were angered by English incursions on their land. In London, the Lords of Trade, deeply alarmed, on September 18 directed the governor of New York to open negotiations with the Iroquois, and also take steps to deal with those who had allegedly defrauded them of their land. He was advised not to approve any future land transactions between private individuals and Indians. Henceforth, the Lords Board of Trade declared, Indian land purchases should be made only by the crown, not by private individuals. They also informed the governor that he should convene a conference with the Iroquois and invite representatives of the other British colonies to attend. Governor Osborne did not live to carry out his instructions, for he died unexpectedly that fall. The task of presiding over a conference of Iroquois and colonial representatives was taken up by James De Lancey, lieutenant governor of New York, who convened a meeting at Albany in June 1754. Several colonies—including Virginia—declined to participate, as did leaders of several of the Iroquois nations. The principal Iroquois spokesman was the Mohawk chief Theyanoguin, whom the British called King Hendrick. Elderly and corpulent, Hendrick was a longtime ally of the English and was closely associated with the Indian agent William Johnson. He joined Johnson in the 1755 offensive against Crown Point, and lost his life in the battle with Baron Ludwig Dieskau's forces. After his death, few Iroquois gave any support to the English until the French defeat was imminent. During the Albany Conference, Hendrick on several occasions explained why the Iroquois were dissatisfied with the English. The selections from the Conference minutes excerpted below are taken from several of Hendrick's speeches, and express both anger with British behavior toward the Indians and disgust with British disunity and weakness.

Last summer we . . . were down at New York to make our complaints, and we thought the Covenant Chain was broken, because we were neglected; and when you neglect business, the French take advantage of it.

It seemed to us that the Governor had turned his back upon the Five Nations, as if they were no more, whereas the French are doing all in their power to draw us over to them.

We told the Governor last summer, we blamed him for the neglect of the Five Nations, and at the same time we told him, the French were drawing the Five Nations away . . . owing to that neglect, which might have been prevented, if proper use had been made of that warning, but now we are afraid it is too late. . . .

For these three years past (then taking a stick and throwing it behind his back) you have thrown us behind your back, and disregarded us, whereas the French are a subtle and vigorous people, ever using their utmost endeavors to seduce and bring our people over to them. . . .

Brethren! As to the encroachments of the French . . . we have made a strict enquiry amongst all our people, if any of them have given the French leave to build the forts you mention, and we cannot find that either any sale has been made, or leave has been given, but the French have gone thither without our consent or approbation nor ever mentioned it to us.

Brethren! The Governor of Virginia and the Governor of Canada are both quarreling over lands which belong to us [in the Ohio valley], and such a quarrel may end in our destruction; they fight over who shall have the land. The Governor of Virginia and Pennsylvania have made paths thro' our country to trade and build houses without acquainting us with it, they should first have asked our consent to build there. . . .

'Tis your fault Brethren that we are not strengthened by conquest, for we would have gone and taken Crown Point [during King George's war], but you hindered us; we had concluded to go and take it, but we were told that it was too late, and that the ice would not bear us; instead of this, you burnt your own fort at Saratoga and run away from it, which was a shame & a scandal to you. Look about your country & see, you have no fortifications about you, no, not even to this City, 'tis but one step to Canada hither, and the French may come and turn you out of your doors. . . .

Look about you and see all these houses full of beaver, and the money is all gone to Canada, likewise powder, lead and guns, which the French now make use of at Ohio. . . .

You were desirous that we should open our minds, and our hearts to you; look at the French, they are fortifying everywhere—but, we are ashamed to say it, you are all like women, bare and open without any fortifications. . . .'

Brethren! We put you in mind in our former speech of the defenceless state of your Frontiers, particularly of this City and of the Country of the Five

Nations. You told us yesterday you were consulting about securing both your-selves & us. We beg you will resolve upon something speedily. You are not safe from danger one day. The French have their hatchets in their hands, both at Ohio and in two places in New England. We don't know but that this very night they may attack you. . . .

Brethren! There is an affair about which our hearts tremble and our minds are deeply concerned; this is the selling of Rum in our Castles [fortified villages]. It destroys many, both of our old and young people. We request of all the Governments here present, that it may be forbidden to carry any of it amongst the Five Nations. . . . We are in great fears about this Rum, it may cause murders on both sides. We don't want it to be forbidden to be sold to us at Albany, but that none may be brought to our Castles. . . .

Brethren! We Mohawks of both Castles . . . request . . . that the people who are settled round about us may not be suffered to sell our people Rum. It keeps them all poor, makes them idle & wicked; if they have any money or goods they lay it out in Rum. . . .

In response to the speeches of Hendrick and other Indian representatives, Lieutenant Governor De Lancey sent this message:

Brethren! You told me your hearts were deeply concerned at the sad effects which may arise from selling Rum in your respective Countries. I will give orders that the Laws already made for the preventing of the sale of this liquor among you be strictly put in execution, and whatever further provision in the law is necessary, I will endeavor it shall be made. . . . As I have given satisfaction with respect to one of your complaints, about your lands, which lay heavy on your minds [reference to Mohawk complaints about a private land purchase adjudicated during the conference], and have assured you that I shall endeavor to do justice to the rest when I come to New York. . . .

Hendrick replied: We hope that you will not fail in the Covenant Chain, wherewith we have mutually bound ourselves, and now solemnly renewed and strengthened.

Source: O'Callaghan and Fernow, eds., *Documents Relative to the Colonial History of the State of New York,* 6:853–83.

Document 5
William Johnson's Recommendations on Countering French Efforts to Win Indian Support, 1754

After listening carefully to the comments of the Indian delegates to the Albany Conference, William Johnson in July 1754 prepared the following recommendations for dealing with French efforts to win over the Iroquois and other Indian nations. Johnson, a veteran Indian trader and diplomat, had a Mohawk wife and had been made sachem of the Mohawk nation. No British colonial had greater credibility among the Iroquois, or a better understanding of Indian affairs. Johnson was disturbed, as was his close associate Chief Hendrick, by New York's recent inaction and by the lack of unity and resolution among the British colonies generally. In his recommendations, Johnson stressed the need for generosity in dealing with Indians, suggested that the government forgo the collection of duties in the Indian trade in order to lower prices of goods, and called for the development of a coordinated, intercolonial Indian policy. Most immediately, Johnson warned that the British fort at Oswego on Lake Ontario must be strengthened. All of the colonies, he argued, should help bear the expense. His recommendations were not implemented, and Fort Oswego fell to the French in 1756.

As the Six Nations and their Allies are doubtless much altered from what they were some years ago, especially since the French have from time to time, without being interrupted, been treating with them . . . I am sorry to say that a partial defection of these States is too manifest. . . . The Six Nations don't like that either the French or English should establish themselves there [in the Ohio valley], it being their best hunting ground; they rather expected that we should assist in keeping and driving the French off, than that we should build forts only to restrain the French from coming further down on upon ourselves. I believe, were the French hindered from settling, we could have treated with them for those lands, as they never refused us the pre-emption which is more pleasing to them being without hostility, than for the French to take them as it were by force and treat them tho' they were conquered.

To enumerate other requisites, necessary to counteract our common enemy, it is to be observed, that there are stores provided for all Indians at Niagara and all other French trading houses and first to the westward, which are not only sold, but given occasionally, as the Indians stand in need of them; such kind of encouragement should be provided for by an allowance to the King's Officer at Oswego (or at any other forts or trading houses that may be built in Indian Country) . . . this allowance should be expended in some clothing . . . given as presents, also arms, ammunition, and particularly provisions to be given to the Foreign Indians [from the west], they being from their long journey thither always in need of them there, and on their return to their own country.

A strict look out at Oswego should be kept to hinder the French from passing up there, up the Onondaga River, among the Six Nations either to trade with or corrupt them. There should be some English residing in every Nation . . . the different governments [colonies] on the continent should do the same. . . . Here I can't help observing that for want of a strict correspondence between the several governments, in regard to Indian affairs, that the Indians must think that there can be no union in our councils, when it has been known more than once, that the Six Nations have been invited to a conference by different colonies at the same time. This looks among the Indians, as tho' our measures were not mutual, and occasions them to be divided in their councils also, being doubtful of our acting with vigor and unanimity against the French. . . .

A further encouragement to more general trade and intercourse with all the Indians far and near at that place [Fort Oswego] . . . a general mart or fair . . . known to them all, might be promoted by taking off the duties, that the traders could afford to undersell the French. A place of such universal importance should be largely supported by the colonies in general, it being of more concern toward the retaining of all the Indians upon the continent in the British interest, than anything yet proposed, that is, a proper Officer at that place with the allowances afore mentioned, a sufficient number of men to resist the French if attacked, and to hinder their passing the Onondaga River on the south side of Lake Ontario, the Fort should be made much larger and stronger than it is at present. It is by its situation capable of being made so strong as to render it impregnable to any attempt the French might have against it.

Source: O'Callaghan and Fernow, eds., *Documents Relative to the Colonial History of the State of New York*, 6:897–99.

Document 6
Braddock's Defeat and James Smith's Adoption

In 1755, an eighteen-year-old Pennsylvanian, James Smith, volunteered to work on a construction crew that was cutting a supply road to support General Edward Braddock's march against Fort Duquesne. Near the site of the future town of Bedford, Smith and a companion were fired upon by a band of Caughnawaga Indians (former Mohawks who now supported France). His friend was killed and scalped. Smith, thrown from his horse, was uninjured. The Indians seized him and forced him to march to Fort Duquesne. There he was subjected to the running of the gauntlet, a ritual in which Indians massed on either side of a narrow corridor flogged a prisoner entering their village. At Fort Duquesne he learned of Braddock's defeat and witnessed the torture and burning of several prisoners. Still suffering from the effects of his beating, Smith was then taken by his captors to an Indian village in Ohio, where he expected to be tortured and killed. Instead, he was adopted as a replacement for a fallen warrior. He escaped four years later and organized a band of rangers to fight for the British in the Indian manner. Later in life, he served as a colonel in the revolutionary army, helped explore Kentucky, settled there in 1788, served in the legislature, and for a time labored as a missionary to the Indians. He published an account of his four years as an Indian in 1799. The excerpt below, which begins just after Smith's arrival as a prisoner at Fort Duquesne, relates news of Braddock's defeat and recounts Smith's adoption by his captors.

The first thing I remember was my being in the fort, amidst the French and the Indians, and a French doctor standing by me, who had opened a vein in my left arm. The interpreter asked me how I did. I told him I felt much pain. The doctor then washed my wounds and the bruised parts of my body with French brandy. As I felt faint and the brandy smelt well, I asked for some inwardly. But the doctor told me, by the interpreter, that it did not suit my case. . . .

Some time after I was visited by the Delaware Indian already mentioned [as being part of the party that captured Smith]. . . . Though he spoke bad English, I found him to be a man of considerable understanding. I asked him if I had done anything that had offended the Indians, which caused them to treat me so unmercifully. He said no, it was only an old custom, like saying how do you do.

I asked him if I should be permitted to remain with the French. He said no—and told me that as soon as I recovered I must not only go with the Indians but be made an Indian myself.

"What news from Braddock's army?" I asked.

He said that the Indians spied on them every day. He showed me, by making marks on the ground with a stick, that Braddock's army was advancing in very close order, and that the Indians would surround them, take to the trees, and (as he expressed it) "shoot 'em down all one pigeon."

Shortly after this, on the ninth day of July, 1755, in the morning I heard a great stir in the fort. As I could then walk with a staff in my hand, I went out and stood by the wall. The Indians were in a huddle before the gate, where there were barrels of powder, bullets, flints, etc., and everyone taking what he suited [needed]. I saw the Indians also march off . . . likewise the French Canadians and some regulars. After viewing the Indians and French in different positions, I computed them to be about four hundred, and wondered that they attempted to go out against Braddock with so small a party. I was then in high hopes that I would soon see them flying before the British troops, and that General Braddock would take the fort and rescue me . . . a runner . . . arrived who said that Braddock would certainly be defeated, that the Indians and the French had surrounded him and were concealed behind trees and in gullies, and kept a constant fire on the English, who fell in heaps. If they did not take to the river which was the only gap and make their escape, the runner . . . said there would not be one man alive before sundown. Sometime after this I heard a number of scalp halloos and saw a company of Indians and French coming in. They had a great many bloody scalps, grenadiers' caps, British canteens, bayonets, etc., with them. They brought the news that Braddock was defeated. . . .

About sundown, I beheld a small party coming in with about a dozen prisoners, stripped naked, with their hands tied behind their backs and their faces and parts of their bodies blacked. These prisoners they burned to death on the banks of the Allegheny opposite the fort.

I stood on the fort until I beheld them begin to burn one of these men. They had him tied to a stake and kept touching him with firebrands, red-hot irons, etc. He screamed in a most doleful manner, the Indians in the meantime yelling like infernal spirits. As this scene was too shocking for me to behold, I retired to my lodgings. . . .

A few days after this the Indians demanded me and I was obliged to go with them. I was not yet well able to march, but they took me in a canoe up the Allegheny River to an Indian town that was the north side of the river about forty miles above Fort Duquesne. Here I remained about three weeks, and then was taken to an Indian town on the west bank on the west branch of the Muskigham, about twenty miles above the forks, which was called Tullihas, was inhabited by Delawares, Caughnawagas, and Mohicans.

The day after my arrival a number of Indians collected about me, and one of them began to pull the hair out of my head. He had some ashes on a piece of bark, in which he frequently dipped his fingers in order to take a firmer hold, and so he went on, as if he had been plucking a turkey, until he had all the hair clean out of my head, except a small spot about three or four inches square on my crown. This they cut off with a pair of scissors, excepting three locks, which they dressed up in their own mode. Two of these they wrapped round with a narrow pleated garter made by themselves for that purpose, and the other they plaited at full length and then stuck full of silver brooches. After this they bored my nose and ears, and fixed me up with earrings and nose jewels. They ordered me to strip off my clothes and put on a breechclout, which I did. Then they painted my head, face and body in various colors. They put a large belt of wampum on my neck, and silver bands on my hands and right arm, and so an old chief led me out into the street and gave the alarm halloo, "Coo-wigh!" several times, repeated quickly. At this, all that were in the town came running and stood around the old chief, who held me by the hand in their midst. As at that time I knew nothing of their mode of adoption, and had seen them put to death all they had taken, and as I never could find that they saved a man alive at Braddock's defeat, I did not doubt that they were about to put me to death in some cruel manner. The old chief, holding me by the hand, made a long speech very loud, and handed me to three young squaws. They led me down the bank into the river until the water was up to our middle. The squaws made signs to me to plunge myself into the water, but I did not understand them. I thought the result of the council was I should be drowned, and these young ladies were to be the executioners. All three took violent hold of me, and for some time I opposed them with all my might, which occasioned loud laughter among the multitude on the bank of the river. At length one of the squaws resorted to speaking a little English (for I believe they began to be afraid of me) and said, "no hurt you!" At this I gave myself up to their ladyships, who were as good as their word. Though they plunged me under water and washed and rubbed me severely, I could not say that they hurt me much.

These young women then led me to the council house, where some of the tribe were ready with new clothes for me. They gave me a new ruffled shirt, which I put on, also a pair of leggings done off with ribbons and beads, likewise a pair of moccasins, and garters dressed with beads, porcupine quills, and red hair—also a tinsel laced cappo [coat]. They again painted my head and face with various colors, and tied a bunch of red feathers to one of the locks they had left on the crown of my head, which stood up five or six inches. They seated me on a bear skin, and gave me a pipe, tomahawk, and pole-cat skin pouch which contained tobacco and dry sumach leaves, which they mix with their tobacco—also flint, steel, and spunk, a kind of dry wood they use as tinder. When I was thus seated, the Indians came in dressed and painted in their grandest manner, as they came in they took their seats and for a considerable time there was a profound silence. Everyone was smoking, but not a word was spoken among them. At length, one of the chiefs made a speech which was delivered to me by an interpreter. . . . "My son, you are now flesh of our flesh and bone of our bone. By the ceremony which was performed this day, every drop of white blood was washed out of your veins. You are taken into the Caughnawago nation and initiated into a warlike tribe. You are adopted into a great family, and now received with great solemnity in the place of a great man. After what passed this day, you are one of us by an old strong law and custom. My son, you have nothing to fear. We are under the same obligation to love, support and defend you that we are to love and defend one another. You are to consider yourself as one of our people."

I did not believe this fine speech, especially that of the white blood being washed out of me, but since that time I have found there was much sincerity in said speech. From that day I never knew them to make any distinction between me and themselves in any respect whatsoever until I left them. If they had plenty of clothing, I had plenty; if we were scarce of provisions, we all shared one fate.

Source: James Smith, *An Account of the Remarkable Occurrences in the Life and Travels of Col. James Smith* (Lexington, KY: J. Bradford, 1799), 9–17.

Document 7
Robert Eastburn's Captivity Narrative

In the early spring of 1756, Robert Eastburn, a Philadelphia blacksmith, joined a trading expedition bound for the English post at Oswego, New York. Shortly after stopping en route at Fort Williams, the traders learned that a French and Indian invasion force nearby had wiped out an English supply column. Billeted outside the fort in an Indian lodge, Eastburn feared for his life. Rather than waiting for the enemy to strike, he chose to accompany a scouting party dispatched by the fort's commandant. The party soon encountered the enemy, and Indian warriors took him prisoner. His life was spared, but Eastburn was subjected to an arduous and at times terrifying overland march to Canada. He remained there for nearly two years, having been adopted by a family of Indian Roman Catholic converts. Unlike James Smith, Eastburn's captivity was brief. After arriving in Quebec, he was ransomed by one of the officers from Fort Oswego, and allowed to return home via England. After his return to Philadelphia in 1757, Eastburn wrote a short book with a long title: A Faithful Narrative, of the Many Dangers and Sufferings, as Well as Wonderful Deliverances of Robert Eastburn, During His Late Captivity Among the Indians: Together with Some Remarks upon the Country of Canada, and the Religion, and Policy of Its Inhabitants, the Whole Intermixed with Devout Reflections. *A Presbyterian deacon, Eastburn was both anti-Catholic and anti-French, but he nonetheless expressed a grudging admiration for both the piety and the tenacity of his white foes. His characterizations of Native Americans also are mixed. His narrative sheds light not only on the treatment of prisoners of war but also on English perceptions of Indians. The selections from his book reprinted below begin with Eastburn's capture and focus on his interactions with the Indians who took him captive and on his views of the French. Of particular interest are his misgivings about the outcome of the war.*

Presently after I was taken, I was surrounded by a great number, who stripped me of my clothing, hat, and neckcloth (so that I had nothing left but a flannel vest without sleeves), put a rope on my neck, bound my arms fast behind me, put a long band round my body, and a large pack on my back, struck me on the head (a severe blow), and drove me through the woods before them: It is not easy to conceive, how distressing such a condition is! In the meantime, I endeavored, with all my little remaining strength, to lift my eyes to God from whom alone I could with reason expect relief. . . .

Their main body, which inclusive consisted of 400 French and 300 Indians [was] commanded by one of the principal Gentlemen of Quebec. . . . The prisoners were so divided, that but few could converse together on our march, and (which was still more disagreeable and disturbing) an Indian, who had a large bunch of green scalps, taken off our men's heads, marched before me, and another with a sharp spear behind, to drive me after him, which means the scalps were very often close to my face, and as we marched, they very frequently every day gave the Dead Shout, which was repeated as many times as there were captives and scalps taken. . . .

The Indians, perceiving that I was unwell and could not eat their coarse food, ordered some chocolate (which they had brought from the carrying place) to be boiled for me, and seeing me eat that, appeared pleased. A strong guard was kept every night. One of our members, weakened by his wounds and unable to keep pace with them, was killed and scalped on the road! I was all the time almost naked, travelling through deep snow and wading through rivers cold as ice! . . .

As soon as we landed at Conasdauga, a large body of Indians came and incompassed us round and ordered the prisoners to sing and dance the Prisoners' Song . . . at the conclusion of which, the Indians gave a shout, and opened the ring to let us run, and then fell on us with their fists, and knocked several down . . . my head was sore with beating, and pained me several days. The squaws were kind to us, and gave us boiled corn and beans to eat, and fire to warm us, which was a great mercy, for I was both cold and hungry. . . .

Our journey . . . continued several days, till we came near Orwegothcy, where we landed almost three miles from the town, on the contrary side of the river, here I was to be adopted, my Father and Mother that I have never seen before were waiting, and ordered me into an Indian house, where I was directed to sit down silent for a considerable time, the Indians appearing very sad, and my Mother beginning to cry, and continued crying aloud for some time, then dried up her tears, and received me for her son, and took me over the river to the Indian town. The next day I was ordered to go to Mass with them but I refused once and again, yet they continued their importunity several days, saying that it was good to go to Mass, but I still refused, and seeing that they could not prevail with me, they seemed much displeased with their new son. I was then sent over the river, to be employed in hard labour, as a punishment for not going to Mass, and not allowed a sight of, or any conversation with my fellow prisoners. . . .

The next day they carried me back to the Indian town, and admitted me to converse with my fellow prisoners, who told me we were all to be sent to Montreal, which accordingly came to pass.

Montreal, at our arrival here, we had our lodging first in the Jesuits' Convent, where I saw a great number of priests, and people that came to confession; after some stay we were ordered to attend, with the Indians, at a Grand Council, held before the head General Vaudreuil [governor of New France]. . . . Here I was informed that some measures were concerted to destroy Oswego. . . . The Council adjourned for another day, then broke up. My Indian Father and Mother took me with them to several of their old acquaintances, who were French, to shew them their lately adopted son; these persons had been concerned with my Father and other Indians, in destroying many English families in their younger days, and boasting about it. After some days the Council again was called, before which several of the Oneida chiefs appeared, and offered some complaint about the French's attacking our Carrying-Place [Fort Oswego], it being their land, but the General laboured to make them easy, and gave them sundry presents of value, which they accepted. After which, I knowing these Indians were acquainted with Captain Williams, at the Carrying Place, sent a letter by them, to let my family and friends know I was yet alive, and longed for redemption, but it never came to hand. . . .

Arrived at Quebec, May 1st. The honorable Colonel Peter Schuyler, hearing of my coming there, kindly sent for me, and after enquiries about my welfare, &c., told me I should be supplied, and need not trouble for support! This public spirited Gentleman, who is indeed an Honour to his Country, did in like manner, nobly relieve many other poor prisoners at Quebec! Here I had full liberty to walk where I pleased, and view the City, which is well situated for strength, but by no means impregnable.

Here, I hope, it will not be judged improper to give a short Hint of the French Governor's conduct. Even in time of peace, he gives the Indians great encouragement to murder and captivate the poor inhabitants on our frontiers. . . . The Governor gave the Indians presents, to encourage them to proceed in that kind of work, which is a scandal to any civilized nation, and which pagans would abhor! . . .

But to hasten to the Conclusion, suffer me with humility and sorrow to observe that our enemies seem to make a better use of a bad Religion, than we of a good one; they rise up long before day in winter, and go through the snows in the coldest seasons, to perform their devotions in the churches, and when it is over, they return to be ready for their work as soon as daylight appears. The Indians are as zealous in Religion as the French. They oblige their children to pray morning and evening . . . are punctual in performing their stated acts of devotion themselves, are still and peaceable in their own families, and among each other as neighbors!

When I compared our manner of living with theirs, it made me fear that the righteous and jealous God (who is wont to make judgment begin in his own House first) was about to deliver us into their hands, to be severely punished for our departure from him; how long has he waited for our return, O that we may therefore turn to him, before his Anger break out into a flame, and there be no remedy!

Our case appears to me indeed very gloomy! notwithstanding our enemies are inconsiderable in number, compared with us; yet they are *united as one man*, while we may be justly compared to a house divided against itself, and therefore cannot stand long, in our present situation.

Source: Robert Eastburn, *A Faithful Narrative, of the Many Dangers and Sufferings, as Well as Wonderful Deliverances of Robert Eastburn, During His Late Captivity Among the Indians: Together with Some Remarks upon the Country of Canada, and the Religion, and Policy of Its Inhabitants; the Whole Intermixed with Devout Reflections* [1758], ed. John R. Spears (Cleveland: Burrow Brothers, 1904), 30–32, 34–36, 42, 47–49, 63, 70–71.

Document 8
Rogers's Rangers Raid on St. Francis, 1759

Robert Eastburn's accusation that the governor of Canada encouraged Indian attacks on noncombatants in the British colonies was not completely unwarranted, but it did provide a very slanted impression of the nature of the French and Indian War. Both sides disregarded the so-called rules of civilized warfare. Among the most ruthless of the British forces were the rangers commanded by the New Hampshire militia officer Robert Rogers. In the following selection from his journals, Rogers, quoting from his correspondence with General Jeffrey Amherst, describes his attack, in the fall of 1759, on St. Francis, a village of Indian Catholic converts on the St. Lawrence River in Canada. Read carefully, this document discloses that Rogers disregarded Amherst's orders not to kill women and children. Rogers's comments about the atrocities committed in the past by the St. Francis Indians were no doubt intended as an indirect justification of the atrocities committed by his command.

Capt. Kennedy . . . had been sent with a party as a flag of truce to the St. Francis Indians, with proposals of peace . . . [the Indians] made him a prisoner with the whole party; this ungenerous inhumane treatment determined the General [Amherst] to chastise these savages with some severity, and in order to do it, I received from him the following orders, viz.

You are this night to set out with a detachment as ordered yesterday, viz., 200 men, which you will take under your command, and proceed to Missiquoi [Missisquoi] Bay, from whence you will march and attack the enemy's settlement on the south side of the river St. Lawrence, in such a manner as you shall judge most effectual to disgrace the enemy, and for the success and honour of his Majesty's arms.

Remember the barbarities that have been committed by the enemy's Indian scoundrels on every occasion, where they had an opportunity of showing their infamous cruelties on the King's subjects, which they have done without mercy. Take your revenge, but don't forget that tho' those villains have dastardly and promiscuously murdered the women and children of all ages, it is my orders that no women or children are to be killed or hurt.

When you have executed your intended service, you will return with your detachment to camp or join me wherever the army may be.

Yours, &c
Jeff. Amherst

Camp at Crown Point
September 13, 1759

To Major Rogers
In pursuance of the above orders, I set out the same evening with a detachment; and as to the particulars, the reader is referred to the letter I wrote to General Amherst upon my return, and the remarks following it.

Copy of my Letter to the General upon my return from St. Francis

Sir,

The twenty-second day after my departure from Crown Point, I came in sight of the Indian town St. Francis in the evening, which I discovered from a tree that I climbed at about three miles distance. Here I halted my party which now consisted of 142 men, officers included, being reduced to that number by the unhappy accident which befell Capt. Williams [accidentally burned in a gunpowder explosion] and several since tiring, whom I was obliged to send back. At eight o'clock in the evening I left the detachment, and took with me Lieut. Turner and Ensign Avery, and went to reconnoiter the town which I did to my satisfaction, and found the Indians in a high frolic or dance. I returned to my party at two o'clock and at three marched it to within five hundred yards of that town, where I lightened the men of their packs and formed them for the attack.

At half an hour before sunrise I surprised the town when they were all fast asleep, on the right, left and center, which was done with so much alacrity by both the officers and the men that the enemy had not time to recover themselves, or take arms for their own defense, till they were chiefly destroyed except some few who took to the water. About forty of my people pursued them, who destroyed such as attempted to make their escape that way, and sunk both them and their boats. A little after sunrise I set fire to all their houses except for one in which there was corn that I reserved for the use of the party.

The fire consumed many of the Indians who had concealed themselves in the cellars and lofts of their houses. About seven o'clock in the morning the affair was completely over, in which time we had killed at least two hundred Indians, and taken twenty of the women and children prisoners, fifteen of whom I let go their own way, and five I brought with me, viz., two Indian boys and three Indian girls. I likewise retook two English captives which I also took under my care.

When I had paraded my detachment, I found I had Capt. Ogden badly wounded in his body, but not so as to hinder him from doing his duty. I had also six men slightly wounded and one Stockbridge Indian killed. . . . I called the officers together, to consult the safety of our return, who were of the opinion there was no other way for us to return with safety but by no. 4 [an isolated British frontier settlement] on Connecticut River,

I marched the detachment eight days in a body that way; and when provisions grew scarce, near Mempremagog [Memphremagog] Lake, I divided the detachment into small companies, putting proper guides to each, who were to assemble at the mouth of Ammonoosuc River, as I expected provisions would be brought there for our relief. . . .

As to other particulars relative to this scout, which your excellency may think proper to inquire after, I refer you to Capt. Ogden, who bears this and has accompanied me all the time I have been out. . . . I am, Sir, with greatest respect,

Your Excellency's most obedient servant
R. Rogers

November 3, 1759

To General Amherst

I cannot forbear here making some remarks on the difficulties and distresses which attended us in this enterprise upon St. Francis, which is situated within three miles of the river St. Lawrence, about half way between Montreal and Quebec. . . . It was extremely difficult while we kept to the water (and which retarded our progress very much) to pass undiscovered by the enemy, who were then cruising in great numbers upon the lake; and had prepared certain vessels, on purpose to decoy any part of ours that might come that way, armed with all manner of machines and implements for their destruction; but we happily escaped their snares of this kind, and landed (as has been mentioned) the tenth day at Missiquoi Bay. . . . Two Indians came upon me in the evening [of the second day] and informed me that about 400 French had discovered and taken my boats, and that about one half of them were hotly pursuing my track. This unlucky circumstance (it may well be supposed) put us into some consternation. Should the enemy overtake us, and we get the better of them in an encounter; yet being so far advanced into their country where no reinforcements could possibly relieve us, and where they could be supported by any numbers they pleased, afforded us little hope of escaping their hands. Our boats being taken cut off all hope of a retreat by them; besides, the loss of our provisions left with them, of which we knew we should have great need at any rate in case we survived, was a melancholy consideration. It was however resolved to prosecute our design at all adventures, and when we accomplished it, to attempt a retreat. . . . We determined it possible to outmarch our pursuers and effect our design upon St. Francis before they could overtake us. We marched nine days through wet sunken ground; the water most of the way near a foot deep, it being a spruce bog. When we encamped at night we had no way to secure ourselves from the water but by cutting the bows of trees, and with them erecting a kind of hammocks. We commonly began our march a little before day, and continued it til after dark at night.

The tenth day after leaving Missiquoi Bay, we came to a river about fifteen miles above the town of St. Francis to the south of it; and the town being on the opposite or east side of it, we were obliged to ford it, which was attended with no small difficulty, the water being five feet deep and the current swift. I put the tallest man upstream, and then holding by each other, we got over with the loss of several of our guns, some of which we recovered by diving to the bottom for them. We had now good dry ground to march upon, and discovered and destroyed the town as before related, which in all probability would have been effected with the loss of no man but the Indian who was killed in the action had not my boats been discovered and our retreat that way cut off.

This nation of Indians was notoriously attached to the French, and had for near a century harassed the frontiers of New England, killing people of all ages and sexes in a most barbarous manner, at a time when they did not in the least suspect them, and to my own knowledge, in six years, carried into captivity, and killed, on the before mentioned frontier, 400 persons. We found in the town hanging on poles over the doors &c, about 600 scalps, mostly English.

The circumstances of our return are chiefly related in the preceding letter. . . .

Source: Robert Rogers, *The Journals of Major Robert Rogers* (London: J. Millan, 1765), 144–54.

Document 9
A Young Militiaman Describes the Defeat at Ticonderoga, 1758

Peter Pond was a Connecticut volunteer who participated in the ill-fated British assault on Fort Carillon (Ticonderoga) in 1758. Despite his lowly rank, Pond clearly understood the folly of General James Abercromby's order that a frontal attack on the fort be mounted before the artillery could be deployed. His account conveys a sense of the common American soldier's contempt for a commander who would first place their lives in great danger in a poorly planned offensive, and then, despite a great numerical advantage over the enemy, abandon the field. Pond survived the war, went west, and earned his living as a fur trader. His journal is one of the most interesting sources of the period. The excerpt reprinted below begins immediately after an account of disorder and confusion during the march to Fort Carillon, and the difficulty of assembling the troops, some of whom got lost in the woods. Pond's account is unpolished, but nonetheless gives us a vivid sense of the human side of a military disaster.

This delay gave the French what they wanted—time to secure their camp, which was well executed. The next day, which was Saturday, about eleven, we were set in motion, the British [troops] leading the van . . . they were drawn up before strong breastworks . . . we had no cannon up [at] the works. The intent was to march over this works but they [the British officers] found themselves sadly mistaken. The French had cut down a great number of pine trees in front of their camp at some distance. While some [of the French] were entrenching, others were employed cutting off the limbs of trees and sharpening them at both ends, others cutting off large logs and getting them ready for the breastwork. At length they were ready for our reception. About twelve of the parties began their fire & the British put their plan on foot to march over the works but the limbs of the trees stuck fast in the ground and all pointed on the upper end that they could not get through them and were at last obliged to quit the plan for three fourths were killed in the attempt. But the greater part of the army laid in the rear on their faces until night while the British were battling a breastwork nine logs thick in some places which was done without the help of cannon though we had as fine an artillery just at hand as could be in an army of fifteen thousand men. But they were of no use while they were lying on their faces. Just as the sun was setting Abercromby came from left to right in the rear of the troops engaged and ordered a retreat beat and we left the ground with about two thousand two hundred lost as I was informed by an officer who saw the return of the wounded and missing. We were ordered to regain our boats at the lake side which was done after travelling all night so slowly we fell asleep by the way. About nine or ten in the morning we were ordered to embark & cross the lake to the head of Lake George. But see the confusion! There was [sic] the soldiers [who] could not find their own boats but embarked promiscuously where ever they could get in, expecting the French on their heels every minute. We arrived at the head of the lake in a short time—took up our old encampment which was well fortified. After a few days the army began to come to themselves and found they were safe, for the hold of the French in that part of the country was not more than three thousand men and we were about forty thousand. We then began to get up provision from Fort Edwards to the camp, but the French were so bold as to beset our scouting party between the camp and Fort Edward and cut off all the teams, destroy the provision, kill the parties, and all under their escort. We passed the summer in that manner, & in the fall very late the camp broke up and what remained went into Winter Quarters in different parts of the colonies. Thus ended the most ridiculous campaign ever heard of.

Source: Charles M. Gates, ed., *Five Fur Traders of the Northwest* (Minneapolis: University of Minnesota Press, 1933), 21–23.

Document 10
Frederick Post's Mission to the Delaware and Shawnee, 1758

Christian Frederick Post, a German-born Moravian missionary, had taken an Indian wife and established close ties with the Indians of the Ohio country. In 1758, Post undertook a hazardous journey into western Pennsylvania that took him deep into French occupied territory. There he endeavored to persuade the Delaware, the Shawnees, and the Mingos to abandon their alliance with France and make peace with Great Britain. He promised that the British would respect their territorial integrity, forget past offenses, and preserve their lives by allowing them to remain neutral in the ongoing war between the French and the English. He urged them to move away from the French and relocate under the protection of the king of England. Post succeeded in convincing some of the chiefs with whom he conferred that the time had come to reconcile with the British. His work, along with the efforts of other forest diplomats such as George Croghan, was instrumental in depriving the French of Indian support and thereby paving the way for General John Forbes's successful assault on Fort Duquesne. But the Indian leaders with whom he negotiated were not hesitant to express their suspicions of both the British and the French. The following excerpt from Post's journal captures some of their exchanges.

[Post addresses Indian delegates]: "Now, brethren at Allegheny, Hear what I have to say. Every one who lays hold of the belt of peace, I proclaim peace to them from the English nation, and let you know that the great King of England does not incline to have war with Indians, but he wants to live in peace and love with them, if they will lay down the hatchet and leave off war against him.

"We love you . . . we let you know that the great King of England has sent a great number of warriors into this country, not to go to war against the Indians in their towns, no, not at all; these warriors are going against the French; they are on the march to the Ohio, to revenge the blood they have shed. And by this belt I take you by the hand, and lead you at a distance from the French, for your own safety, that your legs may not be stained with blood. Come away on this side of the mountain, where we may oftener converse together, and where your flesh and blood lives. We look upon you as our countrymen, that sprung out of the same ground with us; we think, therefore, that it is our duty to take care of you, and we in brotherly love advise you to come away with your whole nation, and as many of your friends as you can get to follow you. We do not come to hurt you, we love you, therefore we do not call you to war, that you may be slain; what benefit will it be to you to go to war with your own flesh and blood? We wish you may live without fear or danger with your women and children . . . if you have any uneasiness or complaint, in your heart or mind, do not keep it to yourself. We have opened the road to the council fire; therefore, my brethren, come and acquaint the Governor with it; you will be readily heard, and full justice will be done you."

After I had done, I left my belts [white wampum, to signify peace] and the strings still before them. The Delaware took them all up, and laid them before the Mingoes, upon which they rose up, and spoke as follows.

Chau: "What I have heard pleases me well; I do not know why I went to war against the English. Moques, what do you think?"

Moques: "You must be strong. I did not begin the war, therefore I have little to say, but whatever you agree to, I will do the same." Then he addressed himself to the Shawanese [Shawnees] and said, "You brought the hatchet to us from the French, and persuaded us to strike our brothers the English; you may consider (laying the belts before them) whatever you have done."

The Shawanese acknowledged they received the hatchet from the French, and persuaded them to strike the English, and they would now send the belts to all the Indians and in twelve days they would meet again. . . .

We set out . . . on the road, Daniel [a Delaware] said, "Damn you, why do not you and the French fight on the sea? You come here only to cheat the Indians and take their land from them. . . . "

Shingas, King Beaver, Delaware George, and Pesqietumen with several other captains (chiefs) said to me, "Brother, we have thought a great deal since God brought you to us, and this is a matter of great consequence, which we cannot readily answer; we will think on it, and will answer you as soon as we can . . . we have great reason to believe that you intend to drive us away, and settle the country, or else, why do you come here to fight in the land that God has given us?"

I said, we did not intend to take the land from them, but only drive the French away. They said, they knew better, for they were informed so by our greatest traders, and some justices of the peace had told them the same thing and the French . . . "tell us the English intend to destroy us, and take our lands, but the land is ours. . . . We love you more than you love us, for when we take any prisoners from you, we treat them as our children. We are poor, yet we clothe them as well as we can, though you see that our children are naked as from the first. By this you may see that our hearts are better than yours. It is plain that the white people are the cause of this war; why do not you and the French fight in the old country, and on the seas? Why do you come to fight on our land? This makes everybody believe you want to take the land from us by force . . . we know there are always a great number of people who want to get rich; they never have enough; look, we do not want to be rich and take away what others have. . . . It is told us, that you and the French contrived the war, to waste the Indians between you, and that you and the French intend to divide the land between you. . . ."

Then I said, "My brothers, I know you have been wrongly persuaded by many wicked people, for you must know, that there are a great many Papists in the country . . . who have put bad notions in your head, and strengthened you against your brothers the English. . . . I beg that you would not believe every idle and false story, that ill designing people may bring to you, against your brothers. . . ."

"I do now declare, before God, that the English never did, nor never will, join with the French to destroy you . . . the French are the beginners of this war. Brothers, about twelve years ago, you may remember, they had war with the English, and they both agreed to articles of peace. The English gave up Cape Breton in Acadia, but the French never gave up the part of the country, which they had agreed to give up; and, in a very little time, made their Children [the Indians] strike the English. This was the first cause of the war. Now, brothers, if any body strike you three times, one after another, you still sit still and consider: they strike you again, then, my brothers, you say, it is time, and you will rise up to defend yourselves. Now, my brothers, this is exactly the case between the French and the English. Consider farther, my brothers, what a great number of our poor back inhabitants have been killed since the French came to the Ohio. The French are the cause of their death, and if they were not there, the English would not trouble themselves to go there. They go no where to war, but where the French are. . . ."

Pisquetumen, Tom Hickman, and Shingas told me "now Brother, we love you, but cannot help wondering why the English and the French do not make up with one another, and tell one another not to fight on our land."

I told them, "Brother, if the English told the French so a thousand times, they would never go away. Brother, you know so long as the world has stood there has never been such a war. You know when the French lived on the other side, the war was there, and here we lived in peace. Consider how many thousand men are killed, and how many houses are burned since the French lived here; if they had not been here, it would not have been so; you know we do not blame you; we blame the French, they are the cause of this war; therefore we do not come to hurt you, but to chastise the French. . . ."

Before I set off, I heard further, that a French captain who goes to all of the Indian towns came to Sacunk, and said, "Children, will you not come and help your father against the English?" They answered, "Why should we go to war against our brethren? They are our friends." "O! Children," said he, "I hope you do not own them for friends." "Yes," they said, "We do, we are their friends and we hope they will remain ours." "O! Children," said he, "you must not believe what you have heard, and what has been told you by that man." They said to him, "Yes, we do believe him more than we do you; it was you that set us against them, and we will by and by have peace with them," and then he said not a word more, but returned to the fort [Duquesne]. So, I hope, some good is done; praised be the name of the Lord.

Source: Reuben Gold Thwaites, ed., *Early Western Travels, 1748–1846*, 32 vols. (Cleveland: Arthur H. Clark, 1904), 1:206–7, 222–24, 227–28.

Document 11
Post Reports the Failure of French Indian Diplomacy, Fall 1758

Christian Frederick Post undertook a second diplomatic mission in the fall of 1758. On October 20, he delivered a message from the governor of Pennsylvania to a group of Indians assembled at a village near Fort Duquesne. He witnessed their response to an appeal from the fort's French commander. Even allowing for Post's bias, his account of the Indians' treatment of the string of wampum that symbolized their war alliance with the French offers vivid evidence of the erosion of Indian support for France.

In the afternoon all the captains gathered together in the middle town; they sent for us, and desired we should give them information of our message. Accordingly we did. We read the message with great satisfaction to them. The number of captains and counselors were sixteen. In the evening messengers arrived from Fort Duquesne, with a string of wampum from the commander; upon which they all came together in the house where we lodged. The messengers delivered the string, with these words from their father, the French King.

"My children, come to me, and hear what I have to say. The English are coming with an army to destroy both you and me. I therefore desire you immediately, my children, to hasten with all the young men; we will drive the English and destroy them. I, as a father, will tell you what is best." He laid the string before one of the captains. After a little conversation, the captain stood up and said, "I have heard something of our brethren the English, which pleaseth me much better. I will not go. Give it to the others, maybe they will go." The messenger took up again the string and said, "He won't go, he has heard from the English." Then all cried out, "Yes, yes, we have heard from the English." He then threw the string to the other fireplace, where the other captains were, but they kicked it from one to another, as if it was a snake. Captain Peter took a stick, and with it flung the string from one end of the room to the other, and said, "Give it to the French captain, let him go with his young men; he boasted much of his fighting; now let us see his fighting. We have often ventured our lives for him; and had hardly a loaf of bread, when we came to him, now he thinks that we should serve him." Then we saw the French captain mortified to the uttermost; he looked pale as death. The Indians discoursed and joked til midnight; then the French Captain at midnight sent messengers to Fort Duquesne.

Source: Reuben Gold Thwaites, ed., *Early Western Travels, 1748–1846*, 32 vols. (Cleveland: Arthur H. Clark, 1904), 1:255–56.

Document 12
Colonel Joseph Frye's Account of the Fort William Henry "Massacre"

British accounts of the killings at Fort William Henry after the surrender did not place sole blame for the atrocities on the Indians. All condemned the French for failing to protect the victims. Some charged Montcalm and his officers with complicity, declaring that the French had encouraged or even ordered the attack. Most greatly exaggerated the number of casualties and omitted mention of French efforts to ransom captives. Some provided their readers with exaggerated, lurid, and often imaginary accounts of Indian abuse of women and children. An early example of successful war propaganda, the Fort William Henry massacre story was transformed by later generations into a rationale for hating Catholics and Indians, and for proclaiming the British victory in the war the triumph of civilization and liberty over savagery and autocracy. Most of the stories of the "massacre" were the work of hack writers who were never at Fort William Henry. An exception is the account in a journal kept by Colonel Joseph Frye of the Massachusetts militia. Finally published in 1819, Frye's eyewitness account is generally regarded as the most authoritative of the English sources. While this document does not support the most extreme claims about the massacre, it does charge that French officers refused to intervene to stop the killings. An excerpt follows.

Wednesday, August 10th.—Early this morning we were ordered to prepare for our march, but found the Indians in a worse temper (if possible) than last night, every one having a tomahawk, hatchett, or some other instrument of death, and constantly plundering from the officers their arms etc. This Col Monro complained of, as a breach of the Articles of Capitulation, but to no effect. The French officers however told us that if we would give up the baggage of the officers and the men to the Indians, they thought it would make them easy, which at last Col Monro consented to but this was no sooner done, then they began to take the officers hats, swords, guns and cloaths, stripping them all to their shirts, and on some officers left no shirt at all, while this was doing they killed and scalp'd all the sick and wounded before our faces and then took out from our troops, all the Indians and negroes, and carried them off, one of the former they burnt alive afterwards.

At last with great difficulty, the troops got out from the retrenchment, they were no sooner out, than the savages fell upon the rear, killing & scalping, which occasioned a halt, which at last was done in great confusion, but as soon as those in front knew what was doing in the rear they again pressed forward, and thus the confusion continued and increased till we came to the Advanc'd Guard of the French, the savages still carrying away officers, privates, women and children, some of which latter they killed and scalped in the road. This horrid scene of blood and slaughter obliged our Officers, to apply to the Officers of the French Guard for protection, which they refused & told them they must take to the woods and shift for themselves which many did, and in all probability many perished in the woods. . . .

Source: The Port Folio, 4th ser. 7 (1819): 365–66.

Document 13
A Jesuit Priest's Account of the Fort William Henry "Massacre"

A different account of the incident at Fort William Henry was written by a Jesuit missionary who had accompanied his Abenaki charges into battle and later, after the fort's surrender, worked hard to persuade the warriors who had seized British soldiers and camp followers to release them. Father Pierre Joseph Antoine Roubaud's letter was published in Paris in 1781 as part of the Jesuit Relations, a collection of missionary documents that ranks as one of the most valuable sources of information on Canada and her Indian peoples in the seventeenth and eighteenth centuries. Father Roubaud testifies that the French tried to restrain the Indians. He portrays the Indians as vicious savages, not acknowledging that their claims on goods and captives were fully consistent with the promises the French had made to them when they were recruited. An excerpt from Father Roubaud's report follows:

At the very dawn of day, the Savages reassembled about the intrenchments. They began by asking the English for goods, provisions,—in a word, for all the riches their greedy eyes could see; but these demands were made in a tone that foretold a blow with a spear as the price of a refusal. The English dispossessed and despoiled themselves, and reduced themselves to nothing, that they might buy at least life by this general renunciation. Such complaisance ought to soften any heart; but the heart of the Savage does not seem to be made like that of other men; you would say that it is, by its nature, the seat of inhumanity. They were not on this account less inclined to proceed to the harshest extremes. The body of four hundred men of the French troops, selected to protect the retreat of the enemy, arrived, and drew up in a line on both sides. The English began to defile. Woe to all those who brought up the rear, or to stragglers whom indisposition or any other cause separated however little from the troop. They were so many dead whose bodies very soon strewed the ground and covered the inclosure of the intrenchments. The butchery, which in the beginning was the work of only a few savages, was the signal which made nearly all of them so many ferocious beasts. They struck, right and left, heavy blows of the hatchet on those who fell into their hands. However, the massacre was not of long continuance, or as great as such fury caused us to fear; the number of those killed was hardly more than forty or fifty. The patience of the English, who were content to bend the head under the sword of their executioners, suddenly appeased the warriors, but did not bring the tormentors to reason and equity. Continually uttering loud cries, these began to take them prisoners. . . .

. . . the main part of our troops, occupied in guarding our batteries and the fort, was, on account of the distance, unable to give them aid. Of what help could four hundred men be against about fifteen hundred furious Savages who were not distinguishing us from the enemy? One of our Sergeants, who had strongly opposed their violence, received a severe wound which brought him to the gate of death . . . Monsieur de Montcalm—who was not apprised of the affair for some time, on account of the distance to his tent—came at the first notice of the place of the uproar, with a celerity which showed the goodness and the nobility of his heart. He seemed to be in several places at once, he would reappear, he was everywhere; he used prayers, menaces, promises; he tried everything, and at last resorted to force. He thought it due to the birth and the merits of Monsieur the Colonel Yonn to rescue his nephew, with authority and with violence, from the hands of a Savage, but alas! His deliverance cost the life of some prisoners whom their tyrants immediately massacred, through fear of a similar action . . .

Such were the circumstances of the unfortunate expedition which dishonored the bravery that the Savages had displayed throughout the course of the siege, and which have made their services burdensome to us. They pretend to justify their deeds—the Abenakis in particular, by the law of retaliation, alleging that more than once in the very midst of peace, or of conferences such as that of last winter, their warriors had come to death by treacherous blows in the English forts in Acadia. . . .

Source: Reuben Gold Thwaites, ed., *The Jesuit Relations and Allied Documents*, 78 vols. (New York: Pageant, 1959), 70:179–80, 183, 195

Document 14
A French Officer Blames Montcalm for the Fall of Quebec, 1759

The fall of Quebec to the invading army commanded by British General James Wolfe in September 1759 signaled the beginning of the end of French control of Canada. Marquis Louis de Montcalm, commander of the French forces defending the city, was an able career soldier, but as a somewhat rigid aristocrat unaccustomed to dealing with either Indians or French Canadians, he experienced some difficulties in adjusting to his new circumstances. His quarrel with the Canadian-born governor, Pierre Vaudreuil, was legendary. Montcalm also made enemies within the ranks. In A Journal Kept at the Army Commanded by the Late Lieutenant General de Montcalm, *written by an anonymous French officer, we find a devastating critique of the general's failure to provide proper coordination of the city's defense. Despite its strong bias against Montcalm, who was mortally wounded in the battle on the Plains of Abraham outside the gates to Quebec, this document offers valuable insights into the reasons for Montcalm's defeat. The excerpt printed below begins just before Wolfe's forces scaled the cliffs below the city.*

September 12. The enemy kept up a very sharp fire the entire day on the town; the [British] fleet, anchored from Cap Rouge as far as Point aux Trimbles, was continually in motion, towards night some vessels were detached from it, which came to an anchor at Sillerie. The movements we saw the enemy making since some time, above Quebec, and the knowledge we had of the character of Mr. Wolf [*sic*], that impetuous, bold, and intrepid warrior, prepared us for a last attack. Such a resolution was really fully adopted in the English army; after breaking up the camp at the Falls, a council of war, as we have since learned from divers English officers, had been held, at which all the general officers voted unanimously in favor of raising the siege; the naval officers observed that the season, already far advanced, was rendering the navigation of the river every day more dangerous, and the officers of the line, disgusted at the tediousness of a campaign, as fruitless as it was difficult, considered it useless to re-main any longer before intrenchments which appeared to them impreg-nable. Both added, moreover, that their army, always a prey to disease, was melting insensibly away. Then, Mr. Wolf [*sic*], seeing that he could not gain anything by openly resisting the general opinion, adroitly took things by the other side. He declared to the members of the council that, so far from differing with them, he was, on the contrary, of their opinion in regard to the inutility of prolonging the siege of Quebec; that therefore in the propo-sition he was about to submit to them, he wished to divest himself of the quality of a general, in order to throw himself entirely on their friendship for him.

"Finally, Gentlemen," he said to them, "as the glory of our arms ap-pears to me to require that we should not retire without making one fi-nal attempt, I earnestly demand of you to be pleased not to refuse your consent thereto; I feel that, in this instance, it is necessary our first steps should place us at the gates of the town. With this view, I am about to try to get a detachment of only one hundred and fifty men to penetrate through the Sellerie woods, and the entire army will prepare to follow. Should this first detachment encounter any resistance on the part of the enemy, I pledge you my word of honor that then, regarding our reputa-tion protected against any sort of reproach, I will no longer hesitate to re-embark."

The zeal that animated so brave a general communicated itself to all the officers who heard him, and nothing was longer thought of in his army but the arrangements necessary for the execution of so noble a plan.

M. de Montcalm, on his side, anxious [to defend] the quarter seem-ingly menaced by the enemy, and fearful, especially, that they intended cutting off our supplies, dispatched additional reinforcements to M. de la Bougainville, who then found that he had under his orders, including Indians, about 300 men, scattered in different posts from Sillerie as far as Point aux Trimbles. 'Twas the elite of the army, in which were reunited all the grenadiers, all the pickets, all the volunteers of the army and the cav-alry: the order to continue to follow, attentively, all the enemy's movements, was reiterated to him. His centre was at Cap Rouge.

Things were in this state, on both sides, when about midnight, be-tween the 12th and the 13th M. Wolf [*sic*] after having, by different move-ments, endeavoured to attract our attention on the Saint Augustin side, sent his barges to fill the post adjoining Sillerie. Fortune appeared in this emergency to combine with the little order which prevailed among our troops, so as to facilitate the approach of these barges.

A convoy of provisions was to come down that same night by water to Quebec; the rumor was circulated all through the posts in front of which it was to pass, without agreeing, among themselves on any rallying cry [password], but some unforeseen event having prevented our bateaux taking advantage of the night tide to sail, their departure was postponed to the following day, and no attention had yet been paid to warn those same posts of the fact. The consequences of this two fold neglect was, that when our sentries saw the enemy's barges advancing, they took them for ours, and satisfied with the word "France" which was returned to the challenge, allowed those barges to pass without giving themselves the trouble to reconnoiter them . . .

The English took advantage of this lapse [in security], landed between two of our posts, and clambered up the precipice they had to ascend, succeeding, by dint of toil, in gaining its crest, where they did not find a soul.

This combination of misfortune and disorder in our service, prepared the final catastrophe, which by a succession of new blunders, in making us lose the fruit of so much fatigue and expense, capped the climax of our humiliation.

So badly established was the communication between each of M. de Bougainville's ports and between the latter and M. de Montcalm's camp, that the English had turned and dispersed about five o'clock in the morning, the detachments which M. de Vergor commanded at l'Aine de Foulon, and were already in order of battle on the heights of Quebec where they even had some field pieces of small calibre, ere any one in our camps was as yet aware that the enemy wished to attack us in that quarter. M. de Bougainville, who was only two leagues off, did not learn that fact, as he says, until eight o'clock in the morning, and M. de Vaudreuil who was at much less than half that distance, was not exactly informed of it until about half past six. The army, which had passed the night in bivouac in consequence of a movement perceptible among the barges at Point Levy, had returned to its tents.

The generale [alarm] was beat; all the troops resumed their arms and followed, in succession, M. de Montcalm, who had repaired to the heights of Quebec where the battalion of Guyenne, which had already returned to our extreme right, was already in position between the town and the enemy whom its presence checked.

In consequence of the corps that had been established from our army at Beauport, the latter found itself since some days reduced to about 6,000 men. The two Montreal battalions composed of about 1,500 men were left to guard the camp; they advanced, however, as far as the River St. Charles when M. de Vaudreuil repaired to the army. M. de Montcalm could, therefore, according to this calculation, muster only 4,500 men.

'Twas with such a feeble force, without affording breathing time to the last detachments which had reached him from our left, and which had run nearly two leagues in one single race, that this General resolved, about one o'clock in the morning, on attacking the enemy (whose light infantry was since some time engaged with ours), on a report he had received, which had not a shadow of a foundation, that the English were busy intrenching themselves.

The rank haste with which M. de Montcalm had made his attack originated in his jealousy. M. de Vaudreuil had, in a note requesting him to postpone the attack until he had reunited all his forces, previously advised him that he was marching in person with the Montreal battalions. . . . [But Montcalm's] ambition was that no person but himself should ever be named [as the savior of Quebec] and this turn of mind contributed not a little to make him thwart . . . enterprises in which he could not appear.

The two armies, separated by a rise of ground, were cannonading one another for about an hour. (Our artillery consisted only of three small field pieces.)

The eminence on which our army was ranged in the order of battle commanded, at some points, that occupied by the English where they were defended either by shallow ravines or by the rail fences of the fields; our troops, composed almost entirely of Canadians impetuously rushed on the enemy, but their ill formed ranks soon broke, either in consequence of the precipitancy with which they had been made to march, or by the inequality of the ground. The English returned our first fire in good order without giving way. They afterwards very briskly returned our fire, and the advance movements made from their centre by a detachment of about 200 men with fixed bayonets, sufficed to put to flight almost the whole of our army.

The rout was total only among the regulars; the Canadians accustomed to fall back Indian fashion (and like the ancient Parthians) and to turn afterwards on the enemy with more confidence than before, rallied in some places, and under cover of brushwood, by which they were surrounded, forced divers corps to give way, but at last were forced to yield to the superiority of numbers. The Indians took scarcely any part in this affair. They kept themselves, for the most part at a distance, until the success of the battle should decide which part they should take. 'Tis well known they never face the enemy in open field.

These particulars, with the aid of a map, will enable a reader to appreciate the blunders committed by M. de Montcalm on the day. The following are the principle [*sic*] ones with which impartial judges unanimously reproach him:

1st. He ought, on learning that the enemy had landed, [to have] dispatched orders to M. de Bougainville, who had, as already stated, the elite of the troops of the army; by combining his movements with those of the Colonel, it . . . [would have] been easy for him to make it impossible for the enemy to avoid finding himself between two fires.

2nd. The fate of Quebec depending on the success of the battle about to be fought, he ought to bring all his forces together. 'Twas useless, therefore, to leave a corps of 1,500 men at our camp, the more especially as being intrenched only on the side of the river, and commanded by ground in the rear covered with timber, it would never be a tenable post for the enemy; besides the batteries which lined it were manned by gunners.

3rd. For the same reason . . . he ought to draw off the pickets on duty there [on the river]; this would have been an addition of 7 to 800 men. He could in like manner, have ordered up the artillery; there was no lack of field pieces.

4th. His army being, in great part, composed only of Canadians, who 'tis known are not adapted to fighting a pitched battle, instead of losing the advantage of the post by going to attack an enemy too well arrayed, he ought to wait and profit by the nature of the ground to place those Canadians by platoons in the clumps of brushwood by which he was surrounded, arrayed in that way, they certainly excel all the troops in the universe by the precision with which they fire.

5th. Being determined on attacking, he ought, at least, to have altered his arrangements . . . the militia had been incorporated among the Regulars. Could any harmony be expected in the movements of a body the different parts of which must, of necessity, by their constitution, mutually embarrass each other?

6th. Finally, he did not dream of forming a corps de reserve . . . the errors committed by M. de Montcalm have been fatal to our arms.

Source: O'Callaghan and Fernow, eds., *Documents Relative to the Colonial History of the State of New York*, 10:1034–41.

Document 15
Pontiac Describes Neolin's Vision, 1763

In 1763, Robert Navarre, a French resident of Detroit who spoke the Ottawa language, recorded some of the speeches delivered by the war chief Pontiac. Pontiac sought to forge a Pan-Indian alliance that would drive the British from the west and restore the old trading relationship with the French. In his exhortations, Pontiac invoked the teachings of the Delaware prophet Neolin, a nativist visionary who condemned all whites. Neolin was not a religious traditionalist. He borrowed freely from the teachings of Christian missionaries to create a new syncretic religion that incorporated European ideas about an omnipotent sky god and about monogamy, monotheism, sin, redemption, heaven, and hell. Neolin used those concepts to support his call for an Indian resistance. His Creator-God loved Indians and hated whites. In the passages below, Pontiac describes Neolin's journey to heaven and his meeting with God, whom he called "the Master of Life." Neolin, in response to a dream, has undertaken a journey to find paradise. After being driven back by pillars of fire blocking two roads, he has traveled for a day down a third, narrower trail.

Suddenly, he saw before him what appeared to be a mountain of marvelous whiteness and he stopped, overwhelmed with astonishment. Nevertheless, he again advanced, firmly determined to see what this mountain could be, but when he arrived at the foot of it he no longer saw any road and was sad. At this juncture, not knowing what to do to continue his way, he looked around in all directions and finally saw a woman of this mountain, of radiant beauty, whose garments dimmed the whiteness of the snow. And she was seated.

This woman addressed him in his own tongue: "Thou appearest to me to be surprised to find any road to lead thee where thou wishest to go. I know that for a long while thou hast been desirous of seeing the Master of Life and of speaking with him; that is why thou hast undertaken this journey to see him. The road which leads to his abode is over the mountain, and to ascend it thou must foresake [*sic*] all thou hast with thee, and disrobe completely, and leave all thy trappings and clothing at the foot of the mountain. No one shall harm thee; go and bathe thyself in a river which I shall show thee, and then thou shalt ascend."

The Wolf [a reference to Neolin's clan affiliation] was careful to obey the words of the woman, but one difficulty yet confronted him, namely, to know how to reach the top of the mountain which was perpendicular, pathless, and smooth as ice. He questioned this woman how one should go about climbing up, and she replied that if he was really anxious to see the Master of Life, he would have to ascend, helping himself only with his hand and his left foot. This appeared to him impossible, but encouraged by the woman he set about it and succeeded by dint of effort.

When he reached the top he was greatly astonished not to see anyone; the woman had disappeared, and he found himself alone without a guide. At his right were three villages . . . he did not know them for they seemed of different construction from his own, prettier and more orderly in appearance. After he had pondered some time over what he ought to do, he set out toward the village which seemed to him the most attractive, and covered half the distance from the top of the mountain before he remembered that he was naked. He was afraid to go further, but he heard a voice telling him to continue and that he ought not to fear, because having bathed as he had, he could go on in assurance. He had no more difficulty in continuing up to a spot which seemed to him to be the gate of the village, and here he stopped, waiting for it to open so he could enter. While he was observing the outward beauty of this village the gate opened, and he saw coming toward him a handsome man, clothed all in white, who took him by the hand and told him he was going to satisfy him and let him talk with the Master of Life. The Wolf permitted the man to conduct him, and both came to a place of surpassing beauty which the Indian could not admire enough. Here he saw the Master of Life who took him by the hand and gave him a hat all bordered with gold to sit down upon. The Wolf hesitated to do this for fear of spoiling the hat, but he was ordered to do so, and obeyed without reply.

After the Indian was seated the Lord said to him: "I am the Master of Life, and since I know what thou desirest to know, and to whom thou wishest to speak, listen well to what I am going to say to thee and to all the Indians:

"I am He who hath created the heavens and the earth, the trees, lakes, rivers, all men, and all thou seest upon the earth. Because I love you, ye must do what I say and love, and not do what I hate. I do not love that ye should drink to the point of madness, as ye do; and I do not like it that ye should fight one another. Ye take two wives, or run after the wives of others. . . . I hate that. Ye ought to have but one wife, and keep her till death. When ye wish to go to war, ye conjure and re-sort to the medicine dance, believing that ye speak to me; ye are mis-taken—it is to the Manitou that ye speak, an evil spirit who prompts you to nothing but wrong, and who listens to you out of ignorance of me.

"This land where ye dwell I have made for you and not for others. Whence comes it that ye permit the Whites upon your lands? Can ye not live without them? I know that those whom ye call the children of your Great Father [the whites] supply your needs, but if ye were not evil, as ye are, ye could surely do without them. Ye could live as ye did live before those whom ye call your brothers came upon your lands. Did ye not live by bow and arrow? Ye had no need of gun or powder, or any-thing else, and nevertheless ye caught animals to live upon and to dress yourselves with their skins. But when I saw that ye were given up to evil, I led the wild animals to the depths of the forests so that ye had to de-pend upon your brothers [the whites] to feed and shelter you. Ye have only to become good again and do what I wish, and I will send the back the animals for your food. I do not forbid you to permit among you the children of your Father [a reference to the French]; I love them. They know me and pray to me, and I supply their wants and all they give you. But as to those who trouble your lands,—drive them out, make war upon them. I do not love them at all; they know me not, and are my enemies, and the enemies of your brothers. Send them back to the lands which I have created for them and let them stay there . . . drive off your lands those dogs clothed in red [the British] who will do you nothing but harm. . . ."

Source: [Robert Navarre], *Journal of Pontiac's Conspiracy*, trans. R. Clyde Ford (Detroit: Clarence Monroe Burton, 1910), 22–30.

ANNOTATED BIBLIOGRAPHY

Primary Sources

O'Callaghan, E.B., and Fernow, B., eds. *Documents Relative to the Colonial History of the State of New York*. 15 vols. Albany, NY: Weed and Parsons, 1853–87. This collection contains a number of documents, some translated from French, that are of value to students of the French and Indian War. Consult vols. 6 and 10.

Pargellis, Stanley, ed. *Military Affairs in North America, 1748–1765: Selected Documents from the Cumberland Papers in Windsor Castle*. New York: Appleton-Century, 1936. Some of the letters, memoranda, and reports in this collection reflect British frustrations in dealing with colonial civil and military officials.

Rogers, Robert. *Rogers' Journals*. New York: Corinth Books, 1966. Fascinating first-hand look at the war through the eyes of the legendary ranger.

Sullivan, John, ed. *The Papers of Sir William Johnson*. 14 vols. Albany: State University of New York, 1921–65. Johnson, a prominent British trader and Indian agent, conducted much of Britain's Indian diplomacy in the northern colonies and served as a commander during the French and Indian War.

Thwaites, Reuben Gold, ed. *The Jesuit Relations and Allied Documents: Travels and Explorations of the Jesuit Missionaries in New France, 1610–1791*. 78 vols. Cleveland: Burrow Brothers, 1896–1901. The indispensable source for students of Indian-French relations in North America, these reports from the Jesuit missionaries to their superiors in France contain much valuable information on the ongoing conflicts with the British.

Thwaites, Reuben Gold, ed. *Early Western Travels 1748–1846*. 32 vols. Cleveland: Arthur H. Clark, 1904. The first volume in this collection includes several journals describing Indian diplomacy in the west during the French and Indian Wars.

VanDerBeets, Richard, ed. *Held Captive by Indians: Selected Narratives, 1642–1836.* Knoxville: University of Tennessee Press, 1973. All of these narratives are useful in understanding Indian-white relations in colonial America. Robert Eastburne's account, reprinted here, offers an intriguing view of French treatment of captives as well.

General Histories

Anderson, Fred. *Crucible of War: The Seven Years' War and the Fate of Empire in British North America.* New York: Alfred A. Knopf, 2000. Best recent study of the subject, this book is particularly strong on the relationship of the war to the problems that led to the American Revolution.

Black, Jeremy. *Eighteenth Century Europe.* New York: St. Martin's Press, 1999. A sound, up-to-date guide to events and trends of the period.

Brecher, Frank W. *Losing a Continent: France's North American Policy, 1753–1763.* Westport, CT: Greenwood Press, 1998. A good general history that offers a readable narrative history of the war and a solid analysis of its European background.

Dorn, Walter L. *Competition for Empire, 1740–1763.* New York: Harper Torchbooks, 1963. First published in 1940, this study of mid-eighteenth-century Europe remains useful.

Eccles, W.J. *The French in North America. 1500–1783.* Rev. ed. East Lansing: Michigan State University Press, 1998. The best available introduction to French colonialism in North America.

Gallay, Alan, ed. *The Colonial Wars of North America, 1512–1763: An Encyclopedia.* New York: Garland, 1996. A remarkably comprehensive collection of articles, many of them dealing with the personalities, places, and battles of the French and Indian War.

Gipson, Lawrence Henry. *The British Empire Before the American Revolution.* 12 vols. New York: Alfred A. Knopf, 1958–70. A massive, fact-filled, and comprehensive history of the first British Empire, these volumes provide not only a wealth of information about events in America but place the North American colonial wars in a worldwide context. Although this work has never been equaled in scope, Gipson's treatment of Indian affairs is somewhat dated, lacking insight into the nature of Native American cultures. But with that caveat, these books are well worth purusing. The volumes of particular value to students of the French and Indian War are *Zones of International Friction: The Great Lakes Frontier, Canada, the West Indies, 1748–1759; The Great War for Empire: The Years of Defeat, 1754–1757; The Great War for Empire: The Victorious Years, 1758–1760; The Great War for Empire: The Culmination, 1760–1763;* and *Triumphant Empire: Storm Clouds Gather in the West, 1763–1766.*

Jennings, Francis. *Empire of Fortune: Crowns, Colonies & Tribes in the Seven Years War in America.* New York: Norton, 1988. A radical revisionist account of the war stressing the incompetence and brutality of the British Establishment, the humanity of Quaker pacifists, and the plight of the Indians.

Leckie, Robert. *"A Few Acres of Snow": The Saga of the French and Indian Wars.* New York: Wiley, 1999. A readable popular history of all four wars.

Nester, William R. *The First Global War: Britain, France and the Fate of North America, 1756–1775.* Westport, CT: Praeger, 1999. A solid, year-by-year history of the war emphasizing its connection to the American War of Independence.

Parkman, Francis B. *Montcalm and Wolfe: The French and Indian War.* New York: Da Capo Press, 1995. Available in many editions, this work, first published in 1884, remains a classic. It must be used with caution by modern readers, however, for its portrayal of both the French and the Indians is highly biased.

Peckham, Howard H. *The Colonial Wars 1689–1762.* Chicago: University of Chicago Press, 1964. This older study of the wars offers a useful factual survey but, like many other works of the period, does not deal adequately with Native American cultures.

Schwartz, Seymour I. *The French and Indian War, 1754–1763.* New York: Castle Books, 1994. A very attractive pictorial history.

Steele, Ian. *War Paths: Invasions of North America.* New York: Oxford University Press, 1994. A succinct study of colonial Indian wars, notable for its understanding of Native Americans.

Taylor, Alan. *American Colonies.* New York: Viking, 2001. A volume in the Penguin History of the United States, this well-written survey of colonial history provides a broad perspective of the interactions of Native Americans and the English, French, Dutch, and Spanish colonizers in North America. Highly recommended.

Williams, Noel St. John. *Redcoats Along the Hudson: The Struggle for North America, 1754–63.* London: Brassey's, 1998. An excellent short history of the war by a retired British army officer.

Specialized Studies

Anderson, Fred. *A People's Army: Massachusetts Soldiers and Society in the Seven Years' War.* Chapel Hill: University of North Carolina Press, 1984. Illuminates not only the workings of the militia system but also the impact of the struggle on New England life and thought.

Aquila, Richard. *The Iroquois Restoration: Iroquois Diplomacy on the Colonial Frontier, 1701–1754.* Detroit: Wayne State University Press, 1983. Provides some very important background history for understanding the role of the Iroquois in the Anglo-French colonial wars.

Axtell, James. *The Invasion Within: The Conquest of Cultures in Colonial North America*. New York: Oxford University Press, 1981. A comparison of English and French colonization, with particular attention to missionary strategies.

Bailey, Kenneth P. *The Ohio Company of Virginia and the Westward Movement, 1748–1792*. Glendale, CA: Arthur H. Clark, 1939. A valuable analysis of the role of land speculators in Anglo-American expansionism in the western regions contested with France.

Beer, George Louis. *British Colonial Policy, 1754–1765*. Gloucester, MA: Peter Smith, 1958. First published in 1907, this study of British policy making during the war remains valuable.

Black, Jeremy. *Britain as a Military Power 1688–1715*. London: University College London Press, 1999. Provides important background for the understanding of the Anglo-French wars.

Black, Jeremy, and Philip Woodfine, eds. *The British Navy and the Use of Naval Power in the Eighteenth Century*. Leicester: Leicester University Press, 1988. Several chapters shed light on the British victory in the Seven Years' War.

Blackburn, Carole. *Harvest of Souls: The Jesuit Missions and Colonialism in North America, 1632–1650*. Montreal: McGill University Press, 2000. An account of French Jesuit missionary activities among the Indians that emphasizes the cultural differences and misunderstandings dividing the two peoples.

Calloway, Colin G. *New Worlds for All: Indians, Europeans and the Remaking of Early America*. Baltimore: Johns Hopkins University Press, 1997. An excellent explanation of the effects of European colonization on Indians and settlers alike.

Delâge, Denys. *Bitter Feast: Amerindians and Europeans in Northeastern North America 1600–64*. Vancouver: University of British Columbia Press, 1993. A very perceptive study of cultural changes during the early years of contact.

Dowd, Gregory Evans. *A Spirited Resistance: The North American Indian Struggle for Unity, 1745–1815*. Baltimore: Johns Hopkins University Press, 1992. A very valuable account of the Native American religious leaders who inspired Indian resistance movements.

Dowd, Gregory Evans. *War Under Heaven: Pontiac, the Indian Nations, and the British Empire*. Baltimore: Johns Hopkins University Press, 2002. An excellent reassessment of the Pontiac insurgency, emphasizing the cultural insensitivity and racist bias of British Indian policy.

Dunnington, Brian Lange. *Siege—1759: The Campaign Against Niagara*. Youngstown, NY: Old Fort Niagara Association, 1986. A solid military history.

Graham, Gerald S. *Empire of the North Atlantic: The Maritime Struggle for North America*. Toronto: University of Toronto Press, 1980. A history of the often neglected but crucial battles for control of the sea routes to the French and British colonies in America.

Griffiths, N.E.S. *The Acadian Deportation: Deliberate Perfidy or Cruel Necessity?* Toronto: Copp Clark, 1969. A volume in the Issues in Canadian History series, this book includes some very interesting documents and articles.

Henretta, James. *"Salutary Neglect": Colonial Administration Under the Duke of Newcastle*. Princeton, NJ: Princeton University Press, 1988. Essential background to understanding the later conflicts between Great Britain and the American colonies.

Hibbert, Christopher. *Wolfe at Quebec*. New York: Longmans, Green, 1959. A close analysis of Wolfe's great campaign.

Jacobs, Wilbur R. *Wilderness Politics and Indian Gifts: The Northern Colonial Frontier, 1748–1763*. Lincoln: University of Nebraska Press, 1950. Explains the cultural meaning of gift giving in Native American diplomacy and its use by British Indian agents.

Jaenen, Cornelius. *Friend and Foe: Aspects of French-Amerindian Cultural Contact in the Sixteenth and Seventeenth Centuries*. New York: Columbia University Press, 1979. Provides very useful background for understanding French-Indian relations.

Kammen, Michael. *A Rope of Sand: The Colonial Agents, British Politics and the American Revolution*. Ithaca, NY: Cornell University Press, 1968. A very important study of the conflicts over colonial administration that led to the American Revolution.

Kopperman, Paul E. *Braddock at the Monongahela*. Pittsburgh, PA: University of Pittsburgh Press, 1977. A good analysis of Braddock's defeat.

Krech, Shepard III. *The Ecological Indian: Myth and History*. New York: Norton. 1999. A survey of research relating to Indian hunting strategies that challenges the claim that Indians never killed more than they could use.

La Pierre, Laurier. *1759: The Battle for Canada*. Toronto: McClelland and Stewart, 1990. A Canadian historian's account of Montcalm's defeat.

Leach, Douglas. *Arms for Empire: A Military History of the British Colonies in North America, 1607–1763*. New York Macmillan, 1973. Contains much valuable information on the evolution of the colonial militia system.

Leach, Douglas. *Roots of Conflict: British Armed Forces and Colonial America, 1677–1763*. Chapel Hill: University of North Carolina Press, 1986. A very useful investigation of a problematic relationship.

McNairn, Alan. *Behold the Hero: General Wolfe and the Arts in the Eighteenth Century*. Montreal: McGill University Press, 1997. A study of artistic representations of the victor at Quebec.

McNeill, John Roberts. *Atlantic Empires of France and Spain: Louisbourg and Havana, 1700–1763*. Chapel Hill: University of North Carolina Press, 1985. A fascinating view of France's great fortress guarding the sea entrance to Canada.

Middleton, Richard. *The Bells of Victory: The Pitt-Newcastle Ministry and the Conduct of the Seven Years' War, 1757–1763*. Cambridge: Cambridge University Press, 1985. A thorough account of the policy changes that made the British victory possible.

Murphy, Orville T. *The Diplomatic Retreat of France and Public Opinion on the Eve of the French Revolution, 1783–1789*. Washington, DC: Catholic University of America Press, 1998. An analysis of the impact of fiscal problems and of military defeat on French foreign policy and on the prestige of the Old Regime.

Nammack, Georgiana. *Fraud, Politics and the Dispossession of the Indians: The Iroquois Land Frontier in the Colonial Period*. Norman: University of Oklahoma Press, 1969. A very revealing account of British mistreatment of a people with whom they were closely allied.

Pares, Richard. *War and Trade in the West Indies, 1739–1763*. London: Frank Cass, 1963. This analysis of the power struggle in the Caribbean helps put the French and Indian War in North America in broader perspective.

Pargellis, Stanley G. *Lord Loudoun in America*. New Haven, CT: Yale University Press, 1933. This book sheds much light on the reasons for the failure of the British offensives in the early years of the war.

Peckham, Howard H. *Pontiac and the Indian Uprising*. Princeton, NJ: Princeton University Press, 1947. A good study, now superseded by Dowd.

Richter, Daniel. *Facing East from Indian Country: A Native History of Early America*. Cambridge, MA: Harvard University Press, 2001. A study of the responses of Native Americans to the growing European presence from the first explorers to the early nineteenth century.

Riley, James C. *The Seven Years' War and the Old Regime in France: The Economic and Financial Toll*. Princeton, NJ: Princeton University Press, 1986. A highly technical but revealing analysis of the impact on France of the financial burden of the war.

Rogers, J. Alan. *Empire and Liberty: American Resistance to British Authority, 1755–1763*. Berkeley: University of California Press, 1974. Traces the opposition to arbitrary measures such as impressment and quartering of troops, associated with the Revolution, which began during the French and Indian War.

Sosin, Jack M. *Whitehall and the Wilderness: The Middle West in British Colonial Policy, 1760–1775*. Lincoln: University of Nebraska Press, 1961. British efforts to control western expansion are probed in depth in this book.

Starkey, Armstrong. *European and Native American Warfare 1675–1815*. Norman: University of Oklahoma Press, 1998. A very useful analysis of the changes in both European and Indian military technology, strategy, and tactics that grew out of frontier encounters in the New World.

Steele, Ian K. *Betrayals: Fort William Henry and the "Massacre."* New York: Oxford University Press, 1990. A well-written, meticulously documented study that provides a judicious, factual account of a very controversial episode.

Stone, Lawrence, ed. *An Imperial State at War: Britain from 1689 to 1815.* New York: Routledge, 1993. A valuable collection of articles on Britain's long series of world wars with France and her allies.

Trigger, Bruce. *Natives and Newcomers: Canada's "Heroic Age" Reconsidered.* Montreal: McGill-Queens University Press, 1985. An excellent study of the early years of French settlement in Canada by the foremost Canadian anthropologist.

White, Richard. *The Middle Ground: Indians, Empires and Republics in the Great Lakes Region, 1650–1815.* New York: Cambridge University Press, 1991. This is a difficult book, but it is also the best available study of the relationships of Indians, the French, and the British in the Old Northwest. White demonstrates that the customary assumptions about European dominance and Indian submission to colonial authority do not apply in the west, and he proposes a new model for understanding interracial interactions in frontier regions.

Biographies

Ambler, Charles H. *George Washington and the West.* New York: Russell and Russell, 1971. First published in 1936, but still very useful.

Ayling, Stanley. *The Elder Pitt, Earl of Chatham.* London: Collins, 1976. A good study of the life of the "Great Commoner" who led Great Britain to victory.

Black, Jeremy. *Pitt the Elder.* New York: Cambridge University Press, 1992. An excellent, up-to-date biography.

Browning, Reed. *The Duke of Newcastle.* New Haven, CT: Yale University Press, 1975. A study of the career of a very important but less able contemporary of Pitt.

Cuneo, John R. *Robert Rogers of the Rangers.* Ticonderoga, NY: Fort Ticonderoga Presses, 1988. The only reliable modern biography of Rogers.

Flexner, James Thomas. *George Washington: The Forge of Experience, 1732–1775.* Boston: Little, Brown, 1965. A highly regarded account of Washington's formative years.

Flexner, James Thomas. *Mohawk Baronet: A Biography of Sir William Johnson.* Syracuse, NY: Syracuse University Press, 1979. The life of Britain's most powerful and successful Indian agent in North America.

Grinnel-Milne, Duncan. *Mad Is He? The Character and Achievement of James Wolfe.* London: Bodley Head, 1963. A critical biography of the controversial and somewhat eccentric general.

Lewis, Meriwether. *Montcalm, the Marvelous Marquis.* New York: Vantage Press, 1961. The only biography of the French general available in English.

Mitford, Nancy. *Madame de Pompadour.* New York: Random House, 1953. A very engaging popular biography of a powerful and notorious woman.

Reilly, Robin. *The Rest Is Fortune: The Life of Major General James Wolfe.* London: Cassell, 1960. A readable popular biography of the conqueror of Quebec.

Wainwright, Nicholas B. *George Croghan: Wilderness Diplomat.* Chapel Hill: University of North Carolina Press, 1959. A solid account of the life of an Indian trader, diplomat, and land speculator who played a key role in thwarting French efforts to control the western Indians.

Web Sites

Historical Sourcebooks. http://www.fordham.edu/halsall. A very extensive collection of primary source materials assembled at Fordham University. Many of the documents included deal with the background, course, and aftermath of the Seven Years' War.

Prairie Fire: Native Americans and Empires in the Old Northwest. http://dig.lib.niu.edu/prairiefire. A collection of both digital images and written texts compiled at Northern Illinois University.

Web Guide to the French and Indian War. http.//www.geocities.com//Athens/Parthenon/1500/fiw. A listing of a number of web sites dealing with various aspects of the war.

INDEX

About the Author

ALFRED A. CAVE is Professor of History at the University of Toledo, Ohio. He is the author of *Jacksonian Democracy and the Historians* (1964) and *The Pequot War* (1996), and numerous articles on early American ethno-history.